CityPack
Barcelona

MICHAEL IVORY

Michael Ivory has written several guides for AA Publishing. He is a seasoned visitor to Spain, sometimes leading groups of landscape architecture students who never fail to be inspired by this exciting city with its vibrant tradition of urban design.

City-centre map continues on inside back cover ←

AA Publishing

Contents

life 5–12

INTRODUCING
  BARCELONA   6–7
CATALAN PERSONALITIES   8
BARCELONA IN FIGURES   9

A CHRONOLOGY   10–11
PEOPLE & EVENTS
  FROM HISTORY   12

how to organise your time 13–22

ITINERARIES   14–15
WALKS   16–17
EVENING STROLLS   18
ORGANISED SIGHTSEEING   19

EXCURSIONS   20–21
WHAT'S ON   22

top 25 sights 23–48

1 PALAU DE PEDRALBES   24
2 MUSEU MONESTIR DE
   PEDRALBES   25
3 GRÀCIA   26
4 PARC GÜELL   27
5 MONTJUÏC   28
6 POBLE ESPANYOL   29
7 MUSEU NACIONAL D'ART
   DE CATALUNYA   30
8 FUNDACIÓ JOAN MIRÓ   31
9 CASA MILÀ   32
10 MANZANA DE LA
   DISCÒRDIA   33
11 MUSEU D'ART
   CONTEMPORANI   34
12 LA RAMBLA   35
13 DRASSANES & MUSEU
   MARÍTIM   36

14 SAGRADA FAMILIA   37
15 PALAU DE LA MÚSICA
   CATALANA   38
16 CATEDRAL   39
17 PLAÇA DEL REI   40
18 PLAÇA SANT JAUME   41
19 MUSEU PICASSO   42
20 SANTA MARIA DEL MAR   43
21 PORT VELL   44
22 PALAU DE MAR   45
23 PARC DE LA CIUTADELLA   46
24 MUSEU D'ART MODERN   47
25 BARCELONETA & PORT
   OLÍMPIC   48

Index 94–95

About this book 4

best 49–60

GALLERIES & MUSEUMS	50–51	CHURCHES	57
MODERNISTA & MODERN		SPORTS & AMUSEMENTS	58
ARCHITECTURE	52–53	ATTRACTIONS FOR	
PARKS & GARDENS	54–55	CHILDREN	59
PLAÇAS	56	WHAT'S FREE	60

where to... 61–86

EAT

OLD CITY	62–63
EIXAMPLE & GRÀCIA	64–65
BARCELONETA & PORT OLÍMPIC	66
UPPER BARCELONA	67
TAPAS BARS & CAFÉS	68–69

SHOP

MALLS & DEPARTMENT STORES	70
ARTS, CRAFTS & DESIGN	71
FASHION	72–73
SHOES & ACCESSORIES	74
BOOKS & MUSIC	75
FOOD SHOPS & MARKETS	76
GIFTS & ANTIQUES	77

BE ENTERTAINED

BARS, DISCOS & CLUBS	78–79
FILM, THEATRE & MUSIC	80–81
POPULAR MUSIC	82
TRADITIONAL ENTERTAINMENT	83

STAY

LUXURY HOTELS	84
MID-RANGE HOTELS	85
BUDGET ACCOMMODATION	86

travel facts 87–93

ARRIVING & DEPARTING	88–89	MEDIA & COMMUNICATIONS	91–92
ESSENTIAL FACTS	89–90	EMERGENCIES	92–93
PUBLIC TRANSPORT	90–91	LANGUAGE	93

CREDITS, ACKNOWLEDGEMENTS AND TITLES IN THIS SERIES	96

About this book

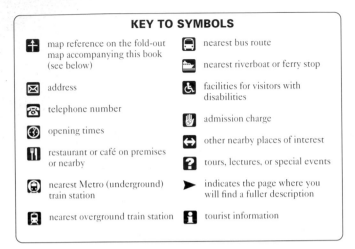
CityPack Barcelona is divided into six sections to cover the six most important aspects of your visit to Barcelona. It includes:

- An overview of the city and its people
- Itineraries, walks and excursions
- The top 25 sights to visit
- Features about different aspects of the city that make it special
- Detailed listings of restaurants, hotels, shops and nightlife
- Practical information

In addition, easy-to-read side panels provide fascinating extra facts and snippets, highlights of places to visit and invaluable practical advice.

CROSS-REFERENCES

To help you make the most of your visit, cross-references, indicated by ➤, show you where to find additional information about a place or subject.

MAPS

The **fold-out map** in the wallet at the back of the book is a comprehensive street plan of Barcelona. All the map references given in the book refer to this map. For example, the Manzana de la Discòrdia on Passeig de Gràcia has the following information: ➕ H7 – indicating the grid square of the map in which the Manzana de la Discòrdia will be found.

The **city-centre maps** found on the inside front and back covers of the book itself are for quick reference. They show the top 25 sights, described on pages 24–48, which are clearly plotted by number (❶ – ㉕, not page number) from west to east.

BARCELONA
life

Introducing Barcelona   6–7

Catalan Personalities   8

Barcelona in Figures   9

A Chronology   10–11

People & Events from History   12

INTRODUCING BARCELONA

Modernisme...

This is the Catalan version of the international movement in art and design known elsewhere as art nouveau, Jugendstil and Secession. Barcelona's claim to pre-eminence is based on the extraordinary number of buildings erected around the turn of the century by immensely talented and original architects; Antoni Gaudí is only the best known. Their designs embraced the advanced technology of steel and glass while reinterpreting the country's Gothic and Moorish architectural heritage.

Phrases like 'Spain's second city' and 'A city of the North in the South' hint at the paradoxes in the character of Barcelona. Far from being simply the focal point of one of Spain's regions, Barcelona is the capital of the Catalan nation, housing historic institutions of state like the Generalitat, the Catalan government. Though Spanish is spoken here, officialdom uses Catalan, the language once used to conduct the commerce of much of the Mediterranean.

There is plenty here to remind you that you are in southern Europe: the long lunch period when many shops and museums are closed, the animation of the evening promenade, and the hot humid nights of summer. In the evenings, locals often meet up with friends and snack on tapas until dinner, which can start as late as 10PM. Then the real nightlife begins as people throng dance clubs, designer bars and other nightspots. The great pedestrian promenade, the Rambla, stays busy until dawn, particularly at weekends, and areas such as Gràcia and the Eixample are favourite spots for those in search of food or fun. This is truly a city that never sleeps, and the opportunities for pleasure seem endless.

Barcelona is busy, colourful and bursting with vitality

Yet Barcelona is as devoted to business as any northern European city. It has a disproportionate share of Spain's industry and commerce, and *Barcelonins* are renowned for their enterprise. Civic pride expresses itself in an array of new parks and squares and an impressive public transport system, while traditional Catalan craftsmanship has provided a foundation for the innovative design which has made Barcelona a centre of post-modern style.

The city is squeezed into a narrow coastal plain between the abrupt escarpment of the Sierra de Collserola and the Mediterranean. It consists of a medieval core, the Barri Gòtic (Gothic Quarter), the city blocks and boulevards of the great 19th-century extension, the Eixample, and a sprawling outer ring of modern residential and industrial suburbs.

Ornate drinking fountain on Rambla de Canaletes

Subjected to rule from Madrid and torn by internal conflict, Barcelona and Catalonia have shared the troubled history of Spain. In the Civil War of 1936–39, the city was the last capital of the ill-fated Spanish Republic, which was defeated by Franco's Nationalists. It made happier appearances on the global stage during the Expositions of 1888 and 1929, whose relics still mark the townscape today. The 1992 Olympics spurred the city to make civic improvements and to promote a progressive image of Barcelona to the world.

That image is undeniably positive. There is international recognition of the city's special contribution to architecture and the design of fashion, furniture, everyday objects, shops, and nightspots. Barcelona, deservedly, has become one of the top European destinations of travelers taking short city breaks, and its style, its urban attractions, its flamboyant nightlife are certain to please.

...and the Modernistas

Apart from Gaudí, the big names in *Modernisme* include Domènech i Montaner and Puig i Cadafalch. Catalan patriots as much as inspired architects, both saw their buildings as total works of art and collaborated with the talented craftsmen Catalonia has always seemed to produce in quantity. Their buildings must be savoured slowly if the richness of their detailed organic decoration and sinuous lines are to be enjoyed to the full.

CATALAN PERSONALITIES

*Catalan tennis star –
Arantxa Sanchez-Vicario*

Arantxa Sanchez-Vicario

Spain's great tennis champion was born in Barcelona in 1971 and still returns home between tournaments. She has won over 75 major tennis titles, including both the French and U.S. Open in 1995.

ANTONI TÀPIES

Born in Barcelona in 1923, Antoni Tàpies introduced contemporary abstract painting into Spain. He gave up his law studies at the University of Barcelona in 1946 to become an artist and two years later co-founded the Surrealist group *Dau al Set* (Seven Sided Die). He later moved away from Surrealism toward more abstract work. In 1990, the Tàpies Foundation opened in Barcelona, displaying over 2,000 of the artist's works.

MONTSERRAT CABALLÉ

The acclaimed soprano, born in Barcelona in 1933, began her music studies at the prestigious Conservatorio del Liceo at an early age. Audiences across the globe have applauded her in roles such as Mimi, in Giacomo Puccini's *La Bohème*, and the Countess in Mozart's *Marriage of Figaro*.

PASQUAL MARAGALL

Leader of the Catalan socialist party and mayor of Barcelona between 1982–1997, Pasqual Maragall was a leading light in Barcelona's 1980s revitalisation. With the injection of public and private investment for the 1992 Olympics, Maragall oversaw massive rebuilding, particularly in the port area. This led to a burst of confidence in the design culture of Barcelona. Maragall remains a part of the Barcelona political scene.

JORDI PUJOL

Imprisoned for Catalanist activities in the 1960s under General Franco's repressive regime, Jordi Pujol won the leadership of the restored Generalitat in 1980, with his party the Convergència i Unió. Pujol is a leading voice in the promotion of Catalan autonomy, culture, language and economic stature.

MARTÍ LLORENS

Winner of the 1991 European Photography Award in Berlin, Martí Llorens experiments with pin-hole techniques and photomontage to create evocative images of Barcelona. He has exhibited internationally but still lives in Barceloneta.

BARCELONA IN FIGURES

Geography and Economy

- Capital of the Autonomous Region of Catalonia and Seat of Generalitat, the regional government.
- Covers an area of 99sq km (metropolitan area 500sq km).
- High points: Montjuïc (192m) and Tibidabo (542m).
- Hottest months: July and August – average temperature 28°C.
- Coldest month: January – average temperature 13°C
- Distances by road: Madrid 686km; French frontier 165km; London 1,425km.
- Produces 20 per cent of Spain's industrial output (engineering, vehicles, textiles, chemicals).
- Biggest employer: SEAT Vehicles.
- More than 4 million overnight stays by visitors to the city.

Population

- Second largest city in Spain, marginally smaller than Madrid.
- Today 1½ million (metropolitan area 3.5 million).
- 235,000 in 1850, 1,280,000 in 1950, 1,745,000 in 1970.
- Half of *Barcelonins* are first- or second-generation immigrants, mostly from southern Spain.
- Incomes 30 per cent above Spanish average.
- Official languages Catalan and Spanish.

Environment

- Lack of city centre green space partly remedied by addition of parks and *plaças*. Currently 53 parks and gardens.
- City centre and inner city among the world's most densely built up areas.
- Since the 1992 Olympics, the city has top facilities for every kind of sport.
- Six metro lines and 83 bus routes.
- Regional, national and international rail links. Proposed station on projected Paris–Madrid TGV line. Main line railways pass beneath the city centre.
- Almost 5km of beach adjacent to city centre, largely artificial.
- Two luxury marinas.

9

A CHRONOLOGY

27BC–AD14	Roman colony of Barcino founded during reign of Emperor Augustus.
Late 3rd/early 4th century	City walls built as a result of attacks by Franks and Alemanni.
415	Visigothic invasion and establishment of Kingdom of Tolosa, predecessor of Catalonia.
717	Arab invasion. Barcelona now Barjelunah.
801	Franks gain control of Barcelona, making it part of Charlemagne's empire.
876	Frankish domain south of Pyrenees ruled by Count Guifré el Pilós (Wilfred the Hairy).
988	Catalonia becomes independent after Franks decline to send support against Moors.
1131–62	Reign of Ramon Berenguer IV and union of Catalonia and Aragon. Barcelona a major trading city.
1213–76	Reign of Jaume I. Conquest of Valencia, Ibiza and Mallorca from Moors. New walls built to defend the growing city.
1354	The legislative council of Catalonia – the Corts Catalans – set up the Generalitat to control the city's finances.
1410	Last ruler of the House of Barcelona, Martí I, dies without an heir. Catalan interests now subject to rule from Madrid, which becomes more interested in transatlantic ventures than the stagnant trade of the Mediterranean.
1462–73	Catalan civil war and deterioration of economy.
1640	Revolt of Els Segadors – the Reapers – against Castilian rule.
1714	Barcelona defeated by French and Spanish troops in the War of the Spanish Succession. Catalonia degraded to a province of Spain. The

	Ciutadella (Citadel) becomes a symbol of Bourbon oppression.
1813	Departure of Napoleonic troops. Subsequent industrial and population growth based on textile manufacturing.
1859	Approval of plan for the Eixample, the grandiose extension of the city beyond the city walls.
1888	Universal Exhibition attracts 2 million visitors.
Late 19th/ early 20th century	Development of the Eixample with many examples of *modernista* buildings.
1909	Setmana Tràgica (Tragic Week), with burning of churches and convents.
1914–18	Barcelona's economy boosted by Spanish neutrality in World War I.
1929	International Exposition transforms Montjuïc.
1931	Catalan Republic declared following exile of King Alfonso XIII.
1936	Army uprising led by Nationalist General Franco defeated by armed workers in Barcelona. Resistance to Franco weakened by internal strife between Communists and Anarchists.
1939	Barcelona falls to Nationalists. Catalan identity and culture crushed during subsequent Franco dictatorship. The Catalan language is banned and the region suffers economic decline. Spain remains neutral during World War II.
1977	Following Franco's death in 1975, restoration of monarchy under Juan Carlos I allows re-establishment of Generalitat as the parliament of an autonomous regional government of Catalonia.
1992	Olympic Games.
2004	Barcelona will host the Universal Forum of Cultures, sponsored by UNESCO.

11

PEOPLE & EVENTS FROM HISTORY

Self portrait of Picasso as a young man, 1899–1900. © Succession Picasso/ DACS 1997

Civil strife

After crushing the army rebellion which set off the Civil War in 1936, Barcelona became the seat of government of the Spanish Republic in 1937, after Madrid and Valencia. The uneasy alliances within the government came apart in the same year; the Communists, hoping to consolidate middle-class support, turned on their comrades in the far-left Worker's Party of Marxist Unification (Partido Obrero de Unificaión Marxista, or POUM). The street-fighting that followed, centred on Plaça de Catalunya and the Rambla, is vividly described in *Homage to Catalonia* by George Orwell, himself a POUM militiaman. Consolidation of Communist power failed to halt the advance of Franco's Nationalists, who marched into Barcelona in January 1939.

ANTONI GAUDÍ

Barcelona's civic identity is intrinsically linked to the unique architecture of Antoni Gaudí (1852–1926). A genius of the *Modernista* movement, renowned for his organic structures and distinctive pinnacles, his best known work is the Sagrada Familia (► 37). While work progressed on this masterpiece, Gaudí was tragically run over by a tram and died unrecognised in hospital. When his identity was discovered, the people of Barcelona lined the streets for his funeral.

PABLO PICASSO

Malaga-born Picasso (1881–1973) lived in Barcelona from the age of 14 until 23. He is said to have considered himself more Catalan than Andalucian and even after he moved to Paris in 1904, he continued to visit Barcelona regularly, until the Civil War curtailed his visits. Museu Picasso (► 42) is rich in paintings from his Barcelona period.

ILDEFONS CERDÀ & THE EIXAMPLE

By the mid-19th century Barcelona was growing beyond its medieval walls. From competing plans for an extension of the city (*eixample* in Catalan), the one drawn up by the engineer Ildefons Cerdà was chosen. Work began in 1860, dividing the 9sq km area of the Eixample into symmetrical blocks and grand boulevards. Today, despite modern developments, Cerdà's plan still defines the form of much of the city, and the Eixample remains a visionary example of urban planning.

ANARCHY

The only country where anarchism has enjoyed mass support as a political creed is Spain. In Andalucia, it attracted landless labourers and in late 19th-century Catalonia, it appealed to industrial workers, who felt abandoned by the Church and politicians. In Barcelona it led to attacks on bishops, military men, and the rich. A spectacular outrage took place during a performance of Rossini's *William Tell* at the Liceu, when Santiago Salvador tossed two devices into the stalls, killing 22 of those sitting in the most expensive seats.

BARCELONA
how to organise your time

ITINERARIES 14–15

La Rambla
The Eixample & Pedralbes
Montjuïc, Barceloneta &
    Barri Gòtic
Sagrada Família & Gràcia

WALKS 16–17

The Eixample
Citadel & Harbour

EVENING STROLLS 18

The Barri Gòtic
Towards Barceloneta

ORGANISED SIGHTSEEING 19

EXCURSIONS 20–21

Montserrat
Sitges
Girona
Wine and Cava

WHAT'S ON 22

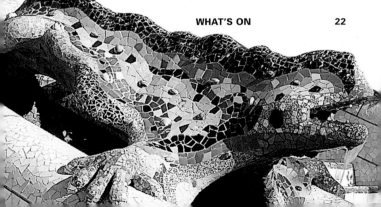

ITINERARIES

Although it is possible to enjoy Barcelona in a weekend, a four-day stay is preferable: the itineraries below cover the major sights. When planning your time, remember that some museums close for siesta between 2PM and 4PM.

ITINERARY ONE	LA RAMBLA
Morning	Stroll down the Rambla (➤ 35) for a good intro-duction to the city. Check out the Boqueria market (➤ 76) on your right and the many flower stalls on the main thoroughfare. A good place to stop for coffee is the Café de l'Opera (➤ 68), opposite the magnificent Grand Teatre del Liceu (➤ 80). Take a detour to get to the Plaça Reial (➤ 56) and the Plaça Sant Jaume (➤ 41).
Lunch	There are plenty of good places to dine in this part of town, including Les Quinze Nits at Plaça Reial 6 (➤ 63).
Afternoon	Return to the Rambla and take a detour down Carrer Nou de la Rambla to see Gaudí's Palau Güell (➤ 53), which opens again after siesta at 4PM. Back on the Rambla, you can continue your walk towards the waterfront. The Museu de Cera (Wax Museum, ➤ 59) on your left is worth a look, or finish off at the excellent Drassanes and Museu Marítim (➤ 36).
ITINERARY TWO	THE EIXAMPLE & PEDRALBES
Morning	From the Passeig de Gràcia catch a No. 22 bus to the Museu Monestir de Pedralbes (➤ 25). Spend some time taking in the calm cloister before visiting the Thyssen-Bornemisza art collection. Walk down Avinguda Pedralbes, and look for Gaudí's gatehouse and dragon gate and then return by bus to the Passeig de Gràcia.
Lunch	There are many convenient lunch stops in this area. Try Citrus at Passeig de Gràcia 44 (➤ 64).
Afternoon	Walk up the Passeig de Gràcia, with its luxury shops and *modernista* buildings – among them, the Manzana de la Discòrdia (➤ 33) and the Casa Milà (➤ 32). Look for the wire sculpture, Cloud and Chair, on top of the Funadció Antoni

Tàpies (► 50). Turning left onto the Rambla Catalunya, take the opportunity to window shop.

ITINERARY THREE	**MONTJUÏC, BARCELONETA & BARRI GÒTIC**
Morning	Go by metro to Paral.lel station, then by funicular to Avenguida de Miramar on Montjuïc (► 28). From here, it's a pleasant walk to the Fundació Joan Miró (► 31) and then on to the Palau Nacional, which houses the Museu Nacional d'Art de Catalunya (► 30) and its collection of Romanesque art. From the MNAC, descend to Espanya metro station and get off at Drassanes before walking along the Passeig de Colom and from there to Barceloneta.
Lunch	Most of the excellent Passeig Joan de Borbó seafood restaurants offer a pricewise *menú del diá*.
Afternoon	Wander back to the Palau de Mar for a visit to the Museu d'Historia de Catalunya (► 45). Then head back through the Barri Gòtic across the Passeig Isabel II. Marvel at the church of Santa Maria del Mar (► 43) and then head along Carrer Argenteria to the cathedral (► 39).
ITINERARY FOUR	**SAGRADA FAMILIA & GRÀCIA**
Morning	Take the metro to Gaudí's celebrated Sagrada Familia church (► 37). Walk to the architecturally interesting Hospital de Sant Pau (► 52).Then head back down Còrsega towards Plaça Joan Carles I and walk up Carrer Gran de Gràcia to see Domènech's Casa Fuster (► 26).
Lunch	This part of town has many bars and restaurants. Try Casa Lorca on the corner of Carrer Lincoln and Carrer Laforja (► 64).
Afternoon	Take a No. 28 bus from Passeig de Gràcia or the Carrer Gran de Gràcia up to the Parc Güell (► 27) for a walk through this extraordinary piece of landscape design. It's then a short downhill walk to village-like Gràcia itself, with its pleasant squares and bars (► 26).

15

WALKS

Detail from the Casa Bruno Quadros in the Ramblas

THE EIXAMPLE

The first part of this day long walk assumes you have already seen the Casa Milà (► 32) and the Manzana de la Discòrdia (► 33), and leads you past some of the lesser-known *modernista* buildings of the Eixample. The Patronat de Turisme's free brochure *Barcelona: Quadrat d'Or* will help you get even more from your morning, but without it you can still enjoy many fine works of architecture in addition to the ones noted here.

Cutting a 45-degree swathe through the grid of the Eixample is the immensely long boulevard aptly named the Diagonal. Plaça Joan Carles I, the important intersection with Passeig de Gràcia, celebrates the role of King Juan Carlos in suppressing the 1981 army *coup d'état*.

Walk eastwards along the Diagonal and turn right into Carrer Roger de Llúria, then left into Carrer de València. Both the church and the market of La Concepció came here in the late 19th century, the medieval church and its cloister brought piece by piece from its original site in the old town.

Go west along Carrer d'Aragó. The crossing with Passeig de Gràcia gives you another chance to admire the extravagances of the Manzana de la Discòrdia and to make a quick visit to the Museu del Perfum. Stay on the south side of Aragó to see the rooftop sculpture of the Fundació Tàpies. Turn left to follow the central pedestrian promenade of Rambla de Catalunya to Plaça de Catalunya. The top-floor cafeteria of El Corte Inglès department store makes an excellent vantage point for lunch.

CITADEL & HARBOUR

The walk takes you through the old streets of the Barri Gòtic to the open spaces and greenery

---

THE SIGHTS

- Casa Comalat (► 52)
- Casa Terrades (► 52)
- Museu del Perfum (► 51)
- Fundació Antoni Tàpies (► 50)

INFORMATION

Distance 2km
Time 2 hours
Start point Plaça Joan Carles I
✚ H6
🚇 Diagonal
End point Plaça de Catalunya
✚ H8
🚇 Catalunya

of the Parc de la Ciutadella and from there it's a short distance to the waterfront.

The short Carrer Rivadeneyra leads from Plaça de Catalunya via a courtyard into Carrer Santa Anna, one of the typical streets of the Barri Gòtic. Continue along Carrer Comtal and cross the busy Via Laietana to the Palau de la Música Catalana. The foyer bar might be a good place to pause in order to absorb the extravagant decoration of this extraordinary building.

Continue along Sant Pere Més Alt to the Plaça Sant Pere with its pretty church before going south to the Plaça Sant Augustí Vell. Find your way down Carrer Carders and then on to Carrer de Montcada, perhaps the city's finest remaining medieval street. A group of its magnificent old palaces houses the Picasso Museum. Come back and turn right onto Carrer Carders, continuing along Carrer Portal Nou to reach the approach to the Parc de la Ciutadella, dominated by the impressive Arc de Triomf built for the 1888 Expo. Opposite is the grandiose Palau de Justícia.

On the far side of Passeig de Pujades is the park itself. The formally laid-out area to the right is a setting for buildings such as the Zoological Museum and the Hivernacle greenhouse, the bar of which is another potential refreshment stop. To the left is the more informal part of the park, including the lake and the Great Cascade.

Leave the park by the exit for Avinguda Marquès de l'Argentera, passing the grand França railway station. From there you can cut back up the Passeig Palau to the magnificent Santa Maria del Mar, Barcelona's finest church, which is surrounded by excellent bars.

THE SIGHTS

- Palau de la Música Catalana (➤ 38)
- Museu Picasso (➤ 42)
- Parc de la Ciutadella (➤ 46)
- Palau de Mar (➤ 45)
- Santa Maria del Mar (➤ 43)

INFORMATION

Distance 3.5km
Time 2 hours and 30 minutes
Start point Plaça de Catalunya
➕ H8
🚇 Catalunya
End point Santa Maria del Mar
➕ H9
🚇 Barceloneta

The Arc de Triomf

EVENING STROLLS

INFORMATION

The Barri Gòtic
Distance About 2km
Time 1 hour
Start point La Rambla
🚌 G9
Ⓜ Liceu
End point Plaça de Catalunya
🚌 H8
Ⓜ Catalunya

Towards Barceloneta
Distance About 2km
Time 1 hour
Start point La Rambla
🚌 G9
Ⓜ Liceu
End point Barceloneta
🚌 H10

Streets and squares

One of the most handsome and famous streets in the world, the Rambla (or Rambles) bisects the old city. Its broad pedestrian promenade, always filled with life, runs for more than 1km from the waterfront to the Plaça de Catalunya. With its labyrinth of underground passageways and metro lines, and constantly swirling traffic, it is the modern hub of the city.

THE BARRI GÒTIC

Soak up the evening atmosphere of the Rambla (► 35) before heading off along Carrer Cardenal Casañas, which leads to the church of Santa Maria del Pi (► 57). The trio of little squares around the church have plenty of restaurants and bars. Carrer de la Palla takes you to the square in front of the cathedral, where Catalonia's national dance, the *sardana*, is performed early on Saturday evenings. Explore the mysterious alleyways to the south of the cathedral before returning to the square and accompanying the crowds promenading up Carrer Arcs and Portal de l'Angel towards Plaça de Catalunya (► 56).

TOWARDS BARCELONETA

Go down the lively Rambla and turn left into the Plaça Reial (► 56), where you can savour the slightly incongruous mixture of tourists, young people intent on fun, and down-and-outs. Go down the passageway at the southern end of the square and turn left into Carrer dels Escudellers. This street has the atmosphere of the medieval city, with its noise, crowds and the chickens roasting on the spit outside the famous Los Caracoles restaurant (► 62). Bear right down the Carrer d'Avinyó, once the haunt of Picasso and his fellow-Bohemians, to the Carrer Ample, where there's a wide selection of tapas bars. Continue to the old port quarter of Barceloneta (► 48), which is also full of places to eat.

The Rambla – buzzing after dark

18

ORGANISED SIGHTSEEING

BUS TURÍSTIC

Easily the best bargain in city sightseeing is the Bus Turístic. There are
two routes, one running north of the
city (red) and the other south (blue);
they connect at Plaça de Catalunya.
Both bus routes have guides on board.
One ticket entitles you to use both
buses all day; you can get on and off as
you please. One- and two-day tickets
(sold on board) entitle you to discounts,
not only on other means of transport
like the Tramvia Blau, the Montjuïc
funicular and the harbour pleasure
boats, but also to sights like the Poble
Espanyol (➤ 29), Fundació Joan Miró (➤ 31)
and the Sagrada Familia (➤ 37).

*City bus proudly flying
the Catalan flag*

City centre stops: Plaça de Catalunya ✚ H8; Passeig de
Gràcia–La Pedrera ✚ H7; Francèsc Macia–Diagonal ✚ F5 🕑 23
Mar–6 Jan daily, every 20 minutes or less. Full tour 3–4 hours
🎫 Inexpensive

GUIDED TOURS

Julià Tours and Pullmantur offer half-day and
whole-day bus tours to principal sights, with
multilingual guides. Prices include some
admission fees. There are also guided visits to
out-of-town destinations like the monastery at
Montserrat (➤ 20) as well as evening tours that
include drinks or dinner and a traditional
flamenco show.

Julià Tours ✉ Ronda Universitat ☎ 93 317 64 54/ 93 317 62 09
Pullmantur ✉ Gran Via de les Corts Catalanes 635
☎ 93 317 12 97

PERSONAL GUIDES

Individual guides can give you a more personal
introduction to Barcelona, either on foot or
by bus.

**Asociación Profesional de Informadores Turísticos
de Barcelona** ✉ Plaça Berenguer el Gran 1 ☎ 93 345 42 21
Barcelona Guide Bureau ✉ Via Laietana 54 ☎ 93 268 24 22
City Guides BCN ✉ Ronda Universitat 21 ☎ 93 412 06
74/93 317 72 00
PSL Cultural Services ☎ 93 301 00 60
Centre d'Informació Plaça Catalunya ☎ 93 304 31 35

Harbour swallows

The opening of the Maremagnum
shopping and entertainment
complex, the general
improvements to the harbour area
and the sprucing-up of the beach
have given the lie to the idea that
Barcelona turns its back on the
Mediterranean. It's fun to take a
boat trip around the harbour, and
to venture even briefly out to sea
on the way to the cafés, shops and
marina of the Port Olímpic
(➤ 48). The double-decker
Golondrines (➤ 59), or swallow-
boats, operate from near the
Columbus Column.

EXCURSIONS

The monastery of Monserrat in its magnificent setting

MONTSERRAT

If you have a day to spare, make the trip to the holy mountain of Montserrat, whose name means 'saw-tooth mountain'. The strangely shaped rock formations rise to more than 1,220m and the surrounding area is a designated nature park, with a rich flora and fauna. But the main reason crowds climb the mountain is to venerate the medieval statue of Our Lady of Montserrat, patron saint of Catalonia, known as the Black Virgin because of the colour of her face. She is displayed above the altar of the monastery church.

The spectacularly sited monastery, founded in 1025 and much rebuilt since then, is still home to monks and has accommodation for pilgrims. The monastery's two museums have Old Master paintings. The church is at its most crowded at 1PM when it is filled with the voices of the monastery's boys' choir. You can escape the throngs by taking a funicular and walking to the hermitage of Sant Joan, or by visiting (also by funicular) the Santa Cova, the cave where legend has it that the Black Virgin was hidden from invading Moors.

SITGES

This old town is among the most attractive of the beach resorts on the coast to either side of Barcelona. Its fine beaches are separated by a low promontory dominated by the parish church. From the mid-19th century, Sitges attracted artists and their hangers-on; the one who left the most lasting impact was the *modernista* painter Santiago Rusiñol, whose villa, the Cau Ferrat, is now a museum. It is filled with a magical mixture of objects with which he surrounded himself – ironwork, traditional ceramics, medieval keys, carvings –

INFORMATION

Montserrat
Distance About 50km west
Journey time About 1 hour and 30 minutes
🚇 Train from Plaça d'Espanya, then cable-car
✉ Monestir
☎ 93 835 02 51
🕐 Basílica 7AM–7:30PM
💶 Basílica free; Museum cheap

Sitges
Distance About 40km southwest
Journey time 30–40 minutes
🚇 Train from Passeig de Gràcia or Sants stations
ℹ Sinea Morera, Sitges
☎ 93 811 76 30

as well as his own collection of paintings and those of fellow artists, including Pablo Picasso. Besides its two other museums, the Palau Mar i Cel and the Museu Romàntic, the latter showing how life was lived by the mid-19th-century rich, Sitges has plenty of *modernista* buildings. The town's somewhat bohemian past gives it a raffish air that has made it popular today with gay travellers.

Church at Sitges

GIRONA

Largely ignored by package tourists, this provincial capital rising over the River Onyar is one of Catalonia's most fascinating historic towns. Its position on the main road from the French frontier made it the subject of many sieges and accounts for its sturdy walls, a good stretch of which remain. The footbridge over the Onyar gives good views of the tastefully painted old houses overlooking the river. Supreme among Girona's several fine churches is the cathedral, whose imposing steps and baroque front conceal a fine medieval interior and Europe's widest Gothic vault. The Banys Arabs, the 13th-century baths probably designed by Moorish craftsmen, are a counterpoint to the old Jewish Quarter, the Call, one of the best-preserved of its kind.

WINE AND *CAVA*

A trip to the Penedés, where Catalan wine (*vi*) and sparkling wine (*cava*) are produced, makes a rewarding day. The principal town, Vilafranca del Penedés, is old and interesting enough in itself, with its arcaded streets, Gothic quarter and excellent Museu de Vi (Wine Museum), housed in a medieval palace. You can observe current production methods at several local wineries, including Bodegues Torres. The town's other claim to fame is the prowess of its castellers, human tower-builders who perform during the *Festa Major* in late August. The *cava* capital is Sant Sadurní d'Anoia; the most prominent producers of this sparkling wine are Freixenet and Codorniu, both of which offer tours and tastings.

INFORMATION

Girona
Distance About 100km northeast
Journey time About 1 hour and 15 minutes
🚆 Train from Passeig de Gràcia or Sants stations
ℹ️ Rambla de la Llibertad 1, Girona
☎ (972) 22 65 75

Vilafranca and Sant Sadurni d'Anoia
Distance About 50km west (Sant Sadurni 40km west)
Journey time About 1 hour (Sant Sadurni 45 minutes)
🚆 Train from Sants or Plaça de Catalunya
ℹ️ Carrer Cort 14, Vilafranca
☎ 93 892 03 58
ℹ️ Plaça de l'Ajuntament 1, Sant Sadurni d'Anoia
☎ 93 891 12 12

21

WHAT'S ON

Barcelona's listings magazines include the weekly *Guía del Ocio*, the Thursday edition of the daily *La Vanguardia* and the monthly *Barcelona: Informació Cultural*; all are in Spanish. The agenda page of the daily *El Pais* is useful, as is the English-language *Barcelona Metropolitan*, a free monthly with listings, available at tourist offices and hotels.

January | *Three Kings* (6 Jan): The kings arrive by boat and shower children with sweets.

February/March | *Carnival*: Boisterous pre-Lenten celebrations include a major costumed procession and the symbolic burial of a sardine. Sitges *Carnival* is particularly colourful.

Easter | Celebrated in style in the city districts with a southern Spanish population.

April | *St George's Day* (23 Apr): The festival of Catalonia's patron saint is marked by lovers' gifts: roses for the woman, a book for the man. There are open-air book fairs and impressive florists' displays.

June/July | *Midsummer* (23–24 Jun): The excuse for mass partying and spectacular firework displays on Montjuïc and Tibidabo. *Festival del Grec* (Jun–Jul): A festival of music, theatre and dance.

August | *Festa Major de Gràcia*: Ten days of street celebrations in the city's most colourful suburb, village-like Gràcia (➤ 26).

September | *Diada de Catalunya* (11 Sep): Flags wave on the Catalan National Day, and political demonstrations are likely. *Festes de la Mercé* (24 Sep): The week-long festival honouring the city's patron saint, Our Lady of Mercy, is Barcelona's biggest. There are musical events, theatre and flamenco performances, parades, fireworks, and spectacles featuring giants, dragons, devils and castellers (human towers).

December | *The Christmas Season*: Preparations include a grand crib in Plaça Sant Jaume (➤ 41) and a market in front of the cathedral.

BARCELONA's
top 25 sights

*The sights are shown on the maps on the inside front cover and inside back cover, numbered **1–25** from west to east across the city*

1 Palau de Pedralbes 24

2 Museu Monestir de Pedralbes 25

3 Gràcia 26

4 Parc Güell 27

5 Montjuïc 28

6 Poble Espanyol 29

7 Museu Nacional d'Art de Catalunya 30

8 Fundació Joan Miró 31

9 Casa Milà 32

10 Manzana de la Discòrdia 33

11 Museu d'Art Contemporani 34

12 La Rambla 35

13 Drassanes & Museu Marítim 36

14 Sagrada Familia 37

15 Palau de la Música Catalana 38

16 Catedral 39

17 Plaça del Rei 40

18 Plaça Sant Jaume 41

19 Museu Picasso 42

20 Santa Maria del Mar 43

21 Port Vell 44

22 Palau de Mar 45

23 Parc de la Ciutadella 46

24 Museu d'Art Modern 47

25 Barceloneta & Port Olímpic 48

PALAU DE PEDRALBES

HIGHLIGHTS

Gardens
- Gaudí's lodge with dragon gate (on C F Primo de Rivera)
- Garden pools and fountains
- Forecourt statue of Queen Isabel II

Museums
- Medieval Mudejar ware
- Ceramic works by Miró and Picasso
- *Modernista* bed of 1908
- Art-deco glass
- 1930–90 Industrial Design Collection

Relaxing in the palace grounds

INFORMATION

- ➕ D4
- ✉ Avinguda Diagonal 686
- ☎ 93 280 50 24
- 🕐 Tue–Sun 10–2
- 🍴 Palau Reial
- 🚌 7, 33, 67, 68, 74, 75
- ♿ Good
- 💶 Moderate; gardens free (ticket admits to both museums)
- ↔ Museu Monestir de Pedralbes (► 25)

When Spanish royals opened the 1888 Expo, bourgeois Barcelona had to lodge them unceremoniously in the town hall. By the time of the second Expo in 1929, the king was able to stay in this fine villa in luxuriant gardens.

Preparing a palace The city fathers' solution to the lack of a proper palace was engineered by J A Güell, son of architect Gaudí's great patron. The grounds of the family's villa in suburban Pedralbes already had a Gaudí gatehouse. In the 1920s, wings were added to the villa, giving it something of the look of a royal palace and the gardens were lavishly landscaped – all in time for King Alfonso's first visit in 1926. The ill-fated monarch came again, in 1929, to participate in the grand opening of the Expo, but with the proclamation of the Spanish Republic in 1931, the palace became city property. During Franco's rule, it was visited no fewer than 14 times by the dictator, who loved the finer things in life. The Generalissimo left no trace of his presence, but a pair of grand thrones grace the otherwise empty Throne Room.

Ceramics and decorative arts The palace was opened to the public in 1960 and is now the splendid setting for a couple of fascinating museums. The superlative collection of the Museu de Ceràmica explores the substantial Spanish contribution to the craft since the 12th century. The displays of the Museu de les Arts Decoratives make a wonderful introduction to the evolution of the decorative arts from the early Middle Ages onwards. The 20th-century exhibits, encompassing *Modernisme* to Minimalism, are ample evidence of Barcelona's claims to pre-eminence in design.

MUSEU MONESTIR DE PEDRALBES

Only a bus ride away from the bustle of central Barcelona stands this serene seat of contemplation, one of Europe's best-preserved and most atmospheric medieval monasteries. It has an excellent collection of Old Master paintings.

Interior of the Church of Monestir de Pedralbes

Monastic museum Once a foothill village outside Barcelona, Pedralbes still exudes a rustic atmosphere, with a cobbled street leading steeply upwards to the fortress-like walls of the great monastery. The nuns first came here in the 14th century and their successors still worship in the austere church. They have had a new residence since 1983, and the historic parts of the monastery have become a fascinating museum of monastic life. The core of the establishment is the superb Gothic cloister, three storeys high, with elegant columns and capitals. In the centre are palms, orange trees' and cypresses; around it are the spaces that once housed varied community activities. The simple cells contrast with the grandeur of the refectory with its vaulted ceiling, and you'll see a pharmacy, an infirmary, the kitchens, the basement storerooms and the great cistern. The chapter house has many mementoes of monastic life, including the funereal urn of Sobirana de Olzet, the first abbess.

The Thyssen-Bornemisza collection After much controversy, Baron Thyssen's magnificent painting collection ended up in Spain. The bulk of it is in Madrid, but the Baron's Catalan wife insisted that some choice canvases come here. The 63 paintings and four sculptures hanging in the splendidly calm dormitory, are mostly religious works by medieval, Renaissance, and baroque masters, a glorious addition to Barcelona's art treasures.

HIGHLIGHTS

Monastery
- Chapel of San Miguel, with 14th-century paintings by Spanish painter and miniaturist, Ferrer Bassa
- Tomb of Queen Elisenda, the monastery's founder
- Dioramas of the *Life of Christ* by Joan Mari

Thyssen Collection
- Fra Angelico, *Madonna of Humility*
- Zubarán, *Christ on the Cross*
- Ceruti, *The Three Beggars*
- Tiziano, *Virgin and Child*
- Veronés, *The Annunciation*

INFORMATION

- ✚ E3
- ✉ Baixada del Monestir 9
- ☎ Monastery 93 203 77 79/93 203 91 16 ; Thyssen Collection 93 280 14 34
- 🕐 Tue–Sun 10–2
- 🚇 Reina Elisenda
- 🚌 22, 63, 64, 75, 78
- ♿ Good
- 🖐 Moderate (separate or combined tickets available)
- ↔ Palau de Pedralbes (➤ 24)

GRÀCIA

HIGHLIGHTS

Casa Vicens
- Elaborate exterior decoration
- Decorative wrought-iron gates

Plaça Rius i Taulet
- Bell tower, designed by Antoni Rovira i Trias

Casa Fuster
- Mix of neo-Gothic and classical styles
- Convex and concave towers

Colourful façade on the Plaça del Sol

INFORMATION

- H5–H6/J5
- Many bars and cafés
- Fontana, Gràcia, Joanic, Plaça Molina
- 22, 24, 28, 39
- Parc Güell (➤ 27)

Barcelona's most distinctive suburb is not only the site of the Parc Güell and a genuine masterpiece from Antoni Gaudí. You'll also find peaceful squares, lively bars and a nine-day street party that attracts more than 2 million each year.

Cultural village From its origins as a collection of tiny farms serving three convents, Gràcia grew rapidly in the 19th century, becoming part of Barcelona itself in 1897. Gràcia was renowned then as a cultural and political centre – a stronghold of republicanism and liberalism and a place where music and theatre thrived. That is still true of the district today. Gràcia boasts the highest concentration of theatres in all of Barcelona, and there are exhibition centres, music societies and cultural spaces of all kinds.

Graceful Gràcia Apart from the Parc Güell, the pick of Gràcia attractions are Gaudí's exquisite Casa Vicens (➤ 52), one of the world's first *modernista* buildings, and Lluis Domènech i Montaner's Casa Fuster (➤ 52). *Plaças* such as Virreina, Sol and Rius i Taulet (➤ 56) are attractive places to pause for thought or stop for a coffee during the day. Boasting some of the best bars and restaurants in the city, Gràcia comes into its own at night.

Summer festival The *Festa Major* has taken place annually for more than 150 years. For nine days during the second half of August, it completely takes over Gràcia. Each street puts up a display, with themes ranging from the Wild West to the Civil War, and the suburb is a riot of colour. You'll also find music, theatre and movies, shown on a giant screen on the Plaça Diamant. The atmosphere is wonderful, and it sometimes seems the whole of Barcelona is here.

PARC GÜELL

Surrealist Salvador Dalí was filled with 'unforgettable anguish' as he strolled among the uncanny architectural forms of this hilltop park, Gaudí's extraordinary piece of landscape design.

Unfulfilled intentions The rocky ridge, which has a magnificent prospect of Barcelona and the Mediterranean, was bought in 1895 by Gaudí's rich patron, Eusebi Güell, with the idea of developing an English-style garden city. The project flopped; only three houses of the proposed 60 were built, and the area was taken over by the city council as a park in 1923.

Anatomy of a park The main feature is the great terrace, supported on a forest of neo-Grecian columns and bounded by a sinuous balustrade-cum-bench whose form was allegedly copied from the imprint left by a human body in a bed of plaster; the surface is covered by fragments of coloured ceramic tiles. The strange space beneath the terrace was intended to be a market; it gapes cavern-like at the top of the steps leading from the park's main entrance.

Surreal landscape A ceramic serpent (or perhaps a dragon) slithers down the stairway towards the main entrance, which is guarded by two ginger-bread-style buildings with bulbous roofs that must be among Gaudí's oddest creations. Gaudí scattered the park with other idiosyncratic details, steps and serpentine paths. He lived in the house built by his pupil Berenguer, now the Casa Museu Gaudí; the museum contains drawings and other memorabilia of the architect.

HIGHLIGHTS

- Boundary wall with ceramic lettering
- Ironwork of entrance gates
- Swelling forms of vaults beneath terrace
- Palm-like stonework of buttresses
- Leaning pillars of arcade
- *Modernista* furnishings in Casa Museu Gaudí

INFORMATION

- ✚ J4
- ✉ Carrer d'Olot
- ☎ 93 213 04 88
- 🕐 May–Aug: daily 9–9. Apr and Sep: daily 9–8. Mar and Oct: daily 9–7. Nov–Feb: daily 9–6
- 🍴 Café
- 📷 Vallcarca (and uphill walk)
- 🚌 25, 28, 87
- ♿ Few
- 🎫 Free

Detail from the Dragon Fountain on the entrance steps

MONTJUÏC

HIGHLIGHTS

Buildings and structures
- Fundació Joan Miró (➤ 31)
- Magic fountains (Plaça Carlos Buigas)
- Parc d'Atraccions de Montjuïc fairground (➤ 58)
- Venetian towers and monumental approach to Palau Nacional

Gardens
- Parc del Fossar de la Pedrera (➤ 54)
- Mossen Costa I Llobera gardens
- Mossen Jacint Verdaguer gardens
- Teatre Grec amphitheatre

Covering an area bigger than the Barri Gòtic, 'Jove's mountain' rises imposingly over the harbour area. This is the city's finest park, a unique assemblage of exotic gardens and tourist attractions, including two of the city's finest museums.

Ancient beginnings Prehistoric people had settled here, high above the harbour, long before the Romans built their shrine to Jove, and the hill's quarries were the source of stone from which half the old city was built. Montjuïc has also always been a place of burial: ancient Jewish cemeteries began a custom of building elaborate tombs, still represented today in the vast Cimenteri del Sud-est on the hill's far flank. Crowning the summit is the castle, which now houses a military museum.

Panoramic views of the city from Montjuïc's cable cars

The 1929 Expo Montjuïc really came into its own in the 20th century. The Expo was preceded by a long period of preparation in which the mountain's slopes were terraced and lavishly planted to create the luxuriant landscape that exists today. Exhibition buildings were put up in a variety of styles ranging from the pompous Palau Nacional (➤ 30) to one of the key works of modern architecture, the Germany Pavilion by Mies van der Rohe (➤ 53). One of the Expo's main attractions was the Poble Espanyol and the great City Stadium was second only to London's Wembley in size. When the Olympic Games came to Barcelona in 1992, Montjuïc became Mount Olympus; the Anella Olímpica (Olympic Ring) includes the splendidly restored stadium as well as its space-age neighbour, the flying-saucer-like Palau de Sant Jordi Japanese architect, Arata Isozaki.

INFORMATION

- ✚ C9, D8/9/10, E8/9/10, F9/10
- 🍴 Several restaurants and cafés
- 🚇 Espanya
- 🚌 13, 61
- 🔁 Poble Espanyol (➤ 29)

POBLE ESPANYOL

Barcelona's 'Spanish Village' provides a whistle-stop tour of the country's architecture and urban scenery. Thousands of tourists crowd here every year to enjoy a trip around the country in a single afternoon.

Virtual reality The Poble Espanyol was one of the star sights of the 1929 Expo, a stunning re-creation of the charm and diversity of Spanish regional architecture. Here are buildings from all the different areas of the country, faithfully re-created by dedicated architects, artists and craftspeople. What might have turned out to be a tacky theme-park experience was so sensitively designed that it has survived, and attracts streams of visitors to this day.

Streets and squares General Primo de Rivera, who was in power during the 1929 Expo, was fanatic about Spanish unity. The Poble Espanyol, a celebration of the rich heritage of the nation as a whole, reflects his vision. It is hard to believe that the entire village, with its perimeter walls, six squares and 3km of streets, was built in just a year. Virtually every style of regional building is represented and blended into a harmonious townscape, from the severe granite structures of rain-swept Galicia, to Mallorcan mansions and the sunny patios of Andalucia. Everywhere there are delightfully photogenic compositions. The village enjoys a life of its own; many buildings house working craftspeople, souvenir shops, cafés, and restaurants, and great efforts have been made to encourage nightlife. Midday on Sundays sees the main square filled with giants, clowns, puppets – and with the children and parents who flock to see them.

HIGHLIGHTS

- Round towers of the Avila Gate
- Ayuntamiento (Town Hall) of Valderrobres in Plaça Mayor
- Santiago stairway
- House from Corella on Plaça Aragonesa
- Mudejar church tower from Utebo
- Church façade from Alcaniz

INFORMATION

- ✚ D/E8
- ⊠ Avinguda del Marquès de Comillas
- ☎ 93 325 78 66
- 🕐 Sun 9–midnight; Mon 9–8; Fri–Sat 9–4; Tue–Thu 9–2
- 🍽 Several restaurants, bars and cafés
- Ⓜ Espanya
- ▭ 13, 61
- ♿ Few
- 💲 Expensive
- ↔ Montjuïc (➤ 28)

Evocative Poble Espanyol

7

MUSEU NACIONAL D'ART DE CATALUNYA

HIGHLIGHTS

- *Stoning of St Stephen* from Sant Joan de Boi (Section 2)
- Wood-carving of Christ of Cerdanya (Section 2)
- Tost Canopy (painting on wood, Section 4)
- Carving of Calvary of Trago de Noguera (Section 4)
- *Christ in Majesty* from Sant Climent de Taüll (Section 5)
- Voussoir from Ripoll (Section 6)
- Carvings of Madonna and Child (Section 8)
- Carving of Christ in Majesty from Battló (Section 8)
- Saints in Torment (Section 10)
- Chapter House from Sigena (Section 21)

Vibrant detail from the Tost Canopy

INFORMATION

- ✚ E8
- ✉ Palau Nacional, Parc de Montjuïc
- ☎ 93 423 71 99
- 🕐 Thu 10–9; Tue, Wed, Fri and Sat 10–7; Sun and hols 10–2:30
- Ⓔ Espanya
- 🚌 13, 61
- ♿ Excellent
- 💷 Moderate
- ↔ Montjuïc (► 28)

No one could fail to notice the colossal and impressive Palau Nacional, which dominates the northern flank of Montjuïc. It houses the National Museum of Catalunyan Art – the Romanesque art collection is a fascinating testament to the region's rich history.

Romanesque riches The climb from Plaça d'Espanya is less formidable than it seems; there are escalators in addition to the steps. Even if there weren't, the art treasures in the Palace would be worth the walk. Catalonia has an exceptionally rich heritage of Romanesque art, created as Christianity recolonised the valleys of the Pyrenees in the 12th and 13th centuries. Powerful images of Christ in Majesty, the Virgin Mary and the saints promoted piety among a peasant population recently released from the Moorish yoke. By the early 20th century, such art enjoyed little prestige, and it was only through heroic efforts of a dedicated band of art historians and archaeologists that so much was saved from decay and theft.

National heritage The collection consists of an extraordinary array of ecclesiastical treasures, as well as sculptures and carvings, but it is the wall paintings that speak to modern sensibilities above all. In an innovative renovation, spaces have been created to replicate the original environment in which these images first worked their magic. Only part of the Palau Nacional has so far been converted, but eventually it will house most of Catalonia's art collections.

Fundació Joan Miró

Poised on the flank of Montjuïc is this white-walled temple to the art of Joan Miró, its calm interior spaces, patios and terraces an ideal setting for the works of this most Catalan of all artists.

Striking tapestry from the Fundació Miró

Miró and Barcelona Born in Barcelona in 1893, Joan Miró never lost his feeling for the city and the surrounding countryside, though he spent much of the 1920s and 1930s in Paris and Mallorca. His paintings and sculptures, with their intense primary colours and swelling, dancing and wriggling forms, are instantly recognisable, but he also gained renown for his expressive ceramics and graphic drawings inspired by political turmoil in Spain. In 1958, he designed a tiled wall for the UNESCO building in Paris. Miró's distinctive influence is visible in graphic work all over Barcelona and locals as well as tourists flock to the Foundation, which is also a cultural centre dedicated to the promotion of contemporary art. It houses changing exhibitions, concerts, a library, excellent shops and a café. Miró's works (10,000 in all, including 217 paintings) are complemented by those of numerous contemporaries including Balthus, Calder, Duchamp, Ernst, Léger, Matisse and Moore.

Mediterranean masterpiece The monumental yet intimate Foundation was built in 1974 by Miró's old friend and collaborator, the architect Josep-Luis Sert, in a style that remains modern, yet traditionally Mediterranean in its use of forms such as domes, arches and roof and floor tiles. It sits easily in the landscape, and its interpenetrating spaces even incorporate old trees like the ancient olive in one of the courtyards. There are glorious views over the city, especially from the roof terrace.

HIGHLIGHTS

- Painting, *The Morning Star*, dedicated to Miró's widow
- *Personage* (1931)
- Surrealist *Man and Woman in front of a pile of excrements*, (1935)
- Barcelona Series (1939–44) Civil War graphics
- Anthropomorphic sculptures on roof terrace
- *Tapis de la Fundació* tapestry (1979)

INFORMATION

- ✝ E9
- ✉ Parc de Montjuïc
- ☎ 93 329 19 08
- 🕐 Jul–Sep: Tue–Sat 10–8 (Thu 10–9:30); Sun and hols 10–2:30. Oct–Jun: Tue–Sat 10–7 (Thu 10–9:30); Sun and hols 10–2:30
- 🍴 Café-restaurant
- Ⓜ Espanya
- 🚌 61
- 🚃 Montjuïc funicular from Paral.lel Metro
- ♿ Good
- ✋ Moderate
- ❓ Bookshop and gift shop
- ↔ Montjuïc (► 28)

CASA MILÀ

HIGHLIGHTS

- Ground floor entrance with wall and ceiling paintings

Espai Gaudí
- Audio-visual show
- Plans and models of major buildings
- Stereofunicular model of building structure
- Gaudí souvenir shop (separate entrance)
- Exhibition space of the Fundació Caixa de Catalunya

INFORMATION

- H6
- Passeig de Gràcia 92
- 93 484 59 00
- Tue–Sat 10–8; Sun 10–3
- Diagonal
- 7, 16, 17, 22, 24, 28
- Good (but not on roof)
- Moderate
- Manzana de la Discòrdia (➤ 33)

Surreal chimneys from the Casa Milà

'Get a violin' was architect Gaudí's brusque response to a resident who wondered where to install a grand piano in this coral reef of an apartment block, which seems designed for slithering sea creatures rather than human beings.

The grotto of the Passeig de Gràcia Anecdotes about the Casa Milà abound: the artist Santiago Rusinyol is supposed to have said that a snake would be a more suitable pet here than a dog. Lampooned for decades after its completion in 1912, this extraordinary building has been rescued from neglect and opened to visitors. Nicknamed La Pedrera (stone quarry), it was built for Pere Milà Camps, a rich dandy who afterwards complained that Gaudí's extravagance had reduced him to penury. The steel frame that supports the seven-storey structure is completely concealed behind an undulating outer skin of stone bedecked with balconies whose encrustations of ironwork resemble floating fronds of seaweed. Obscured from the street, the rooftop undulates too, and in rain and high winds gives a good impression of a ship in a stormy sea.

One of Gaudí's greatest Gaudí originally proposed a spiral ramp that would bring cars to the apartment doors – an impractical idea as it turned out – but the Casa Milà nevertheless had one of the world's first underground garages. The building's beautifully brick-vaulted attics have become the Espai Gaudí, whose weird exhibits make it the best place in Barcelona to learn about Gaudí's work.

MANZANA DE LA DISCÒRDIA

A century ago, the bourgeoisie of Barcelona vied with each other in commissioning ever more extravagant apartment blocks. The most extraordinary of these ornament the Block of Discord on Passeig de Gràcia.

Enlivening the Eixample In an attempt to relieve the rigidity of Cerdà's grid of streets, *modernista* architects studded the Eixample with some of the most exciting urban buildings ever seen. *Modernisme*, the uniquely Catalan contribution to turn-of-the-century architecture (➤ 52), has obvious links with art nouveau, but here it also breathes the spirit of nationalism and civic pride because Barcelona was the richest city in Spain. The Manzana de la Discòrdia juxtaposes the work of the three great architects of the age.

No. 35 Domènech i Montaner completed the six-storey Casa Lleó-Morera in 1905. Much of the interior and exterior of this corner building was destroyed during improvements in the 1940s, but its striking *modernista* style and curved balconies have survived.

No. 41 Built in 1898 by Puig i Cadafalch, the Casa Amatller has an internal courtyard and staircase like the medieval palaces along Carrer Montcada. Outside, it is a wonderful mixture of Catalan Gothic and Flemish Renaissance, faced with coloured tiles and topped by a big gable.

No. 43 The Casa Batlló reflects the hand of Antoni Gaudí, who remodelled the house in 1906. It is said to represent the triumph of St George over the dragon with its heaving roof (the dragon's back), scaly skin of mosaic tiles, windows (the bones of victims), and tower (the saint's lance).

HIGHLIGHTS

No. 35
- Exterior sculptures
- Dome perched on columns

No. 41
- Sculpture of St George and dragon by entrance
- Grotesque sculptures in second-floor windows
- Lamps and stained-glass panels in entrance

No. 43
- Chromatic designs on facade by Gaudí's collaborator, the artist Josep Maria Jujol

INFORMATION

- H7
- Passeig de Gràcia 35,41,43
- Interiors not open to public
- Passeig de Gràcia
- 7, 16, 17, 22, 24, 28
- Casa Milà (➤ 32)

Gaudí's Casa Batlló

MUSEU D'ART CONTEMPORANI

HIGHLIGHTS

Works in the collection (not necessarily on show) by
- Miquel Barceló
- Jean-Michel Basquiat
- Joseph Beuys
- Antoni Clavé
- Xavier Grau
- Richard Long
- Robert Rauschenberg
- Antoni Tàpies

INFORMATION

✚ G8

✉ Museum, Plaça dels Angels 1; Centre, Montalegre 5

☎ Museum 93 412 08 10; Centre 93 481 00 69

◷ Museum Mon–Fri 11–7:30 (closed Tue); Sat 10–8; Sun and hols 10–3. Exhibitions at Centre Wed and Sat 11–8; Sun and hols 11–7; Tue, Thu and Fri 11–2, 4–8

Ⓜ Catalunya, Universitat

🚌 9, 14, 24, 38, 41, 50, 54, 55, 58, 59, 64, 66, 91, 141

♿ Good

💷 Moderate

↔ La Rambla (➤ 35)

Could this be Barcelona's answer to Paris's Centre Pompidou? A glittering white home for late 20th-century art, known as the MACBA, has given the run-down inner city district Raval an ultra-modern shot in the arm.

A modern museum For many years Barcelona felt the lack of an adequate establishment devoted to the contemporary visual arts. During the repressive Franco years, the city found it difficult to keep in touch with the international avant-garde, while its own progressive artists enjoyed little official encouragement. Now two major institutions are bringing it back into the mainstream. By any reckoning, the Museum of Contemporary Art is remarkable, though its long white walls and huge size are strikingly at odds with the ramshackle, dun-coloured façades of its neighbours across the plain modern *plaça* in a less smart part of town. The shining new structure, designed by the American architect Richard Meier, opened in 1995. Its exhibition spaces lead on to a great atrium and are reached by a spectacular series of ramps and glass-floored galleries, sometimes almost upstaging the works on display. Temporary exhibitions featuring local and international artists complement the museum's own extensive collection, which is exhibited in rotation.

Centre de Cultura Contemporànea Housed in the strikingly adapted old monastery buildings of the Casa de la Caritat, the Centre for Contemporary Culture promotes a whole range of activities focused on cultural and social themes. In 2000 and 2001, these include a programme of theatre exploring modern lifestyles and a series of events celebrating radio in Barcelona.

LA RAMBLA

Supreme among city strolling spaces, the Rambla stretches seductively from Plaça de Catalunya to the waterfront. Venerable plane trees frame the broad pavement, which teems with activity at all hours.

Pedestrian paradise Most Catalan towns have their Rambla, a promenade where people go to see and be seen. None, however, enjoys the worldwide fame of Barcelona's. Sooner rather than later, every visitor joins the crowds along this vibrant central space, where strollers rule and traffic is confined to either side. More than a mere thoroughfare, the Rambla is a *place* – somewhere to linger, to sit, to rendezvous, to watch street entertainers, to buy a paper, to simply breathe in the essence of the city. (Until the 18th century, breathing deeply was highly inadvisable; the Rambla owes its origin to an open sewer along the line of the city walls which once stood here).

More than one Rambla The Rambla changes its name several times on its way down towards the Columbus Column, just over 1km from Plaça de Catalunya. First comes Rambla de Canaletes with its famous drinking fountain and well-stocked news kiosks, then Rambla dels Estudis, named for the university once sited here. The Rambla de Sant Josep is also known as Rambla de les Flors, after its profusion of flower stalls. The halfway point is marked by Miró's colourful mosaic in the pavement and by Liceu metro station, named after the city's opera house. The Rambla dels Caputxins follows, with its cafés, then the Rambla de Santa Monica, which has retained its earthy charm despite attempts at modernisation.

HIGHLIGHTS

Starting at Plaça de Catalunya
- Bird and pet market (centre)
- Baroque Betlem Church (right) (► 57)
- 18th century Palau Moja bookshop and cultural centre (left)
- 18th-century Palau de la Virreina information centre (right)
- La Boqueria covered market (right) (► 76)
- Metal dragon on umbrella shop (left)
- Centre d'Art Santa Monica (right)
- Museu de Cera (Wax Museum, left) (► 59)

Detail from a modernista *shop front*

INFORMATION

- ✚ G8/9
- Ⓜ Catalunya, Liceu, Drassanes
- 🚌 91
- ↔ Drassanes (► 36), Port Vell (► 44)

35

DRASSANES & MUSEU MARÍTIM

HIGHLIGHTS

- Medieval navigation charts
- Displays on 19th-century submarine *Ictineo*
- Figurehead collection
- Fishing caravel of 1907

Great Adventure of the Sea

- Catalan Seapower in the 19th century
- Steamships and Emigration
- The Submarine World

INFORMATION

- ✚ G9
- ✉ Avinguda de les Drassanes
- ☎ 93 318 32 45
- 🕐 Tue–Sun 10–7. Closed 1 Jan, 1 May, 24 Jun, 24–25 Dec
- 🍴 Café
- Ⓓ Drassanes
- 🚌 14, 36, 38, 57, 59, 64, 91
- ♿ Few
- 💷 Moderate
- ↔ La Rambla (► 35), Port Vell (► 44)

Magnificent reproduction of the Galera Real

Cut off from today's harbour by cobbled quaysides, the Gothic buildings of the Royal Shipyards are an evocative reminder of Barcelona's longstanding affair with the sea, as well as a unique monument of the Middle Ages. Today, they house the excellent Maritime Museum.

Cathedral of the sea By the 13th century, Catalan sea power extended over much of the western Mediterranean. These ships were built in the covered Royal Shipyards, or Drassanes, a series of long parallel halls with roofs supported on high arches. The effect is of sheer grandeur – of a great cathedral rather than a functional workspace.

Ships on show The Drassanes are now a fascinating museum, displaying charts, model ships and all kinds of maritime memorabilia as well as a number of boats. These are all upstaged by the *Galera Real*, a full-size reproduction of the galley from which Don Juan d' Austria oversaw the defeat of the Turkish navy at the Battle of Lepanto in 1571. Built to commemorate the 400th anniversary of the battle, this elegant vessel is nearly 60m long. The original was propelled to victory at high speed by chained galley slaves. You can see statues of some of them, along with the commander, who stands in the ornate stern, from a high catwalk, which also gives you a fair view of the building itself. Housed in a large exhibition hall, the *Galera Real* forms part of an exciting multimedia exhibit, The Great Adventure of the Sea. Here, gales howl, decks tilt, sirens sound, and visitors descend to the seabed. Through visual and acoustic effects, Catalonia's seafaring history is brought vividly to life.

SAGRADA FAMILIA

George Orwell thought Gaudí's great Temple of the Holy Family one of the ugliest buildings he ever saw, and wondered why the Anarchists hadn't wrecked it in the Civil War. Today it is an emblem of the city.

Devoted designer A must on every visitor's itinerary, Barcelona's most famous building is a mere fragment of what its architect intended. The ultra-pious Gaudí (► 12) began work in 1883, and for the latter part of his life dedicated himself utterly to building a temple that would do penance for the materialism of the modern world. There was never any expectation that the great structure would be completed in his lifetime; his plan called for 18 high towers dominated by an even taller one, an amazing 170m high, dedicated to Jesus Christ. What he did succeed in completing was one of the towers, the major part of the east (Nativity) front, the pinnacled apse, and the crypt, where he camped out during the last months of his life before he was run down and killed by a tram. Ever since, the fate of the building has been the subject of sometimes bitter controversy.

Work in progress Many *Barcelonins* would have preferred the church to be left as it was at Gaudí's death, a monument to its inimitable creator. This view seems to have been at least partly shared by the Anarchists during the Civil War; they destroyed Gaudí's models and drawings though they spared the building itself. But enthusiasm for completion of the project was revived in the 1950s. Work has continued, though opponents strongly believe that attempting to reproduce Gaudí's unique forms in modern materials can only lead to the creation of pastiche.

HIGHLIGHTS

- Crypt museum
- Controversial contemporary sculpture on Passion façade
- Lift or stairway into tower (not for the fearful)
- Symbolic sculptures of Nativity façade

INFORMATION

- J6/7
- Plaça Sagrada Família
- 93 455 02 47
- Apr–Aug: daily 9–8. Mar, Sep and Oct: daily 9–7 Nov–Feb: daily 9–6
- Sagrada Família
- 10, 19, 33, 34, 43, 44, 50, 51
- Expensive (additional charge for lift)

Stonework showing the Annunciation

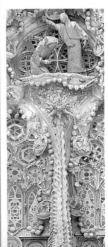

PALAU DE LA MÚSICA CATALANA

HIGHLIGHTS

Main façade
- Catalan songsters in mosaic
- Composers' busts
- Corner sculpture *Allegory of Catalan Folksong*
- Foyer vaults with floral capitals
- Lluis Millet Room
- Bust of Pau (Pablo) Casals (given 1936)
- Modern statue of Millet conducting (outside new entrance)

INFORMATION

- ⊞ H8
- ✉ Sant Francesc de Paula 2
- ☎ 93 268 10 00
- 🕑 Telephone for guided visits, available Mon–Sun 10:30–3, every 30 minutes. Closed Aug
- 🍴 Bar
- Ⓜ Urquinaona
- 🚌 17, 19, 40, 45
- ♿ Good
- 💰 Moderate
- ↔ Catedral (► 39)

Extravagant decoration on the Palau de la Música Catalana

For nearly a century, this glittering jewel has served not only as a concert hall but also as an icon of Catalan cultural life. The sheer profusion of ornament is staggering – a delight in itself.

Domènech's delights The sumptuous Palace of Catalan Music was designed by the great *modernista* architect Domènech i Montaner as the home of the Catalan national choir, the Orfeó. It was inaugurated in 1908 to unanimous acclaim and became a symbol of the new renaissance in Catalan culture. Montaner gave the building a steel frame to support profuse interior and exterior decoration intended to inspire and instruct. This decoration was the work of his own ceramicists, painters, glassworkers, tilers and sculptors.

Art-full auditorium Riches encrust the main façade, the entrance hall, the foyer and staircase, but the 2000-seat concert hall is even more ornate. Light pours in through the transparent walls and from the roof, from which hangs an extraordinary bowl of stained glass. The proscenium arch, far from being a static frame, seems to swell and move, such is the dynamism of its pale pumice sculptures. On the left, a willow tree shelters the great mid-19th-century reviver of Catalan music, Josep Anselm Clavé; on the right a bust of Beethoven is upstaged by Wagnerian Valkyries rollicking through the clouds. Equally stunning is the curving wall at the back of the stage, from which emerge the 18 Muses of music. It's worth the trouble to book in advance for one of the weekly concerts; apart from the splendour of the building, the acoustics are superb.

CATEDRAL

Barcelona's great 14th-century cathedral is one of the finest examples of the Catalan Gothic style. It is a noble successor to its Romanesque predecessor and an even older early Christian basilica built on the site of the Roman forum.

City church Dedicated to an early Christian virgin and martyr, Eulàlia, the cathedral stands firmly at the epicentre of city life. At weekends people gather to dance the elegant *sardana* (► 60), a stately Catalan folk dance which symbolises unity. Inside, worshippers easily outnumber tourists. The cloister is a calm refuge from the city with its magnolias, tall palms, fountain and gaggle of geese.

Medley of styles
The cathedral was begun at the very end of the 13th century and was completed, except for the main façade, by the middle of the 15th. However, it was not until the mid-19th  century that sufficient funds had been accumulated to construct its façade – fashionable but somewhat incongruous in its French-Gothic style. You could spend hours peering at the sometimes faded treasures in the 29 chapels. The most fascinating of these is the old chapter house to the right of the main entrance; beneath a roof rising 20m into a star vault is the Christ of Lepanto, a life-size figure carried into the thick of the famous naval battle aboard the royal flagship (► 36).

HIGHLIGHTS

- Crypt with alabaster tomb of St Eulàlia
- Late medieval and Renaissance choir stalls
- Tomb of 11th-century Ramon Berenguer I
- Museu Capitular (cathedral museum)

Cloister
- Ironwork screens of chapels
- Tomb slabs in floor
- Chapel of St Lucia

Plaça de la Seu
- Picasso's graffiti on College of Architects building

Barcelona's cathedral in the Barri Gòtic

INFORMATION

- ✠ H9
- ✉ Plaça de la Seu
- ☎ 93 315 15 54
- ◷ Cathedral Mon–Fri 8–1:30, 4–7:30; weekends 8–1:30, 5–7:30. Cloister daily 9–1:15, 4–7. Choir Mon–Fri 10–1, 4–7; Sat 10–1
- Ⓜ Jaume I
- 🚌 17, 19, 40, 45
- ♿ Good
- 💶 Cathedral and cloister free; Choir moderate
- ➡ Plaça del Rei (► 40)
- ❓ Occasional access to tower and roof

39

PLAÇA DEL REI

HIGHLIGHTS

Museu d'Història de la Ciutat
- 15th-century courtyard with stairway
- Maps showing city growth
- 16th-century Great Clock

Saló del Tinell
- Traces of late 13th-century wall-painting

Chapel of St Agatha
- 15th-century altarpiece by Jaume Huguet
- City panorama from King Martí's watchtower

INFORMATION

- ✚ H9
- ☎ 93 315 11 11
- 🕐 Tue–Sat 10–2, 4–8 (Jul–Sept 10–8); Sun and hols 10–2
- Ⓜ Jaume I
- 🚌 17, 19, 40, 45
- ♿ Poor
- 🎟 Moderate. Tickets admits to museum, Roman remains, Saló del Tinell, chapel and tower
- ↔ Catedral (➤ 39)
- ❓ Souvenir and bookshop (entrance Carrer Llibreteria)

Nowhere in Barcelona can the antiquity of the city be experienced as intimately as in the Roman settlement of Barcino, the underground world that extends beneath the medieval palace and the Plaça del Rei.

Remains of Roman Barcelona The centre of Roman Barcelona lies in the area extending beneath Plaça Sant Jaume and Plaça del Rei, while chunks of its walls protrude in a number of other places. One of the best-preserved section faces Plaça Ramon Berenguer el Gran, adjacent to Plaça del Rei; above the Roman wall and towers are later layers of building, including the austere medieval Chapel of St Agatha.

Museu d'Historia de la Ciutat The City History Museum's exhibits trace Barcelona's evolution from Roman trading post to metropolis. The museum on Plaça del Rei occupies a medieval palace moved here in 1931 when the Via Laietana was driven through the Barri Gòtic. Remains of the old Roman town were revealed by excavations carried out during the rebuilding work. Mosaic floors and parts of surrounding walls are among the underground ruins accessible from the museum. Other relics from Barcelona's history include statues and an oil press.

Regal relics Back in the Plaça del Rei, which is fairly sombre except during open-air concerts, you can admire the outside of the buildings that make up the medieval palace. But for the real feel of the epoch, go inside, into the splendidly arched space of the 14th-century Saló del Tinell, the banqueting hall where Columbus was received on his return from the New World. Also visit the Chapel of St Agatha and climb the five storey lookout tower Mirador del Rei Martí, named after King Martí.

PLAÇA SANT JAUME

The sardana danced here every Sunday evening is one expression of Catalan culture; other symbols of Catalan identity and aspiration are the palaces facing each other across the square, the Generalitat and the Ajuntament.

Provincial parliament The *plaça* – for centuries the site of a church and a cemetery – is one of the focal points of city life. Here demonstrations and processions wind up, and many a historic speech has been made, including the proclamation of the short-lived Catalan Republic in 1931. The Palau de la Generalitat, on the north side of the square, is the home of the regional government, successor to the Corts Catalanes of the medieval kingdom of Catalonia and Aragon. Begun in the 14th century, the building housing the Palau de la Generalitat has several features celebrating St George, the patron saint of Catalonia; the chapel is named after him, and there's a medieval George over the 15th-century façade on Carrer Bisbe Irurita and a more modern George on the frontage overlooking the square. Only on St George's Day (23 April) does the Generalitat admit visitors.

City Hall The Ajuntament or Casa de la Ciutat, the seat of city government, is more eager to show off its treasures. Beyond the 19th-century main façade, the courtyard retains the feeling of a medieval palace. Stairways lead to an open gallery off which opens the exquisite 14th-century Saló de Cent (Room of the Hundred). From here, the semi-democratic Consell de Cent (Council of the Hundred) ruled Barcelona like a city-state for nearly five centuries.

HIGHLIGHTS

Ajuntament
- Original medieval side façade
- Courtyard sculptures by Miró, Gargallo, Subirachs
- Tiles with craft implements (Saló de Cent)
- Council Chamber (off Saló de Cent)
- Mural of Catalan scenes (on stairway)
- Saló de Croniques with historical murals by Sert

Exterior of Generalitat

INFORMATION

Ajuntament
- H9
- 93 402 70 00
- Weekends 10–2
- Liceu, Jaume I
- 14, 17, 19, 38, 40, 45, 59, 91
- Good
- Free
- La Rambla (➤ 35), Plaça del Rei (➤ 40), Catedral (➤ 39)
- Concerts in the Saló de Cent

41

MUSEU PICASSO

HIGHLIGHTS

- Ceramics from 1940s and 1950s
- *Barceloneta Beach* (1896)
- *Science and Charity* (1897)
- *La Nana* (The Dwarf), 1901
- *El Loco* (The Madman), 1904
- *Harlequin* (1917)
- *Las Meninas suite* (1957)
- Cannes paintings of landscapes and doves (late 1950s)

INFORMATION

- ✚ H9
- ✉ Carrer Montcada 15–19
- ☎ 93 319 63 10
- 🕐 Tue–Sat and hols 10–8; Sun 10–3
- 🍴 Café-restaurant
- Ⓜ Jaume I
- 🚌 14, 16, 17, 19, 36, 39, 40, 45, 51, 57, 59
- ♿ Good
- 🅸 Moderate
- ↔ Santa Maria del Mar (► 43)
- ❓ Large souvenir shop

Las Meninas: *detail.*
© Succession/DACS
1977

Picasso, the greatest painter of modern times, came to live in Barcelona at the age of 14. Many of his formative experienes took place in the old town, so it is appropriate that a museum devoted to his work should be here.

Picasso's palace The Picasso Museum's collection, though extensive, concentrates on certain periods of Picasso's life and artistic evolution, including his time in Barcelona. The work benefits enormously from its setting; the magnificent Palau Berenguer d'Aguilar and two adjacent buildings give an excellent idea of the lifestyle enjoyed by the rich merchant families at the height of medieval Barcelona's prosperity.

At home and away An Andalucian hailing from Malaga, Pablo Ruiz Picasso accompanied his art teacher father and family to Barcelona in 1895. He could already draw like an angel and his skills flourished at his father's academy and later, at art school in Madrid. Beginning in 1899, he immersed himself in bohemian Barcelona, frequenting the red-light district centred on Carrer d'Avinyó, the inspiration for his innovative *Demoiselles d'Avignon* (1907). He became an habitué of Els Quatre Gats (Four Cats), a café where he designed the menu as well as sketching the clientele of artists and barflies. His first exhibition was held here in 1900, the year he made his first visit to Paris. France was to be his real home after that, but he returned to Barcelona many times, and much of the work in his Blue Period (*c*1902–4) was carried out here. The Civil War, which provoked one of his most passionate and controversial paintings, *Guernica* – now housed at the Centro Nacional de Arte Reina Sofía in Madrid – put an end to these visits.

SANTA MARIA DEL MAR

A fortress of the faith in the old port quarter of the Ribera, the Church of Our Lady of the Sea is one of the greatest expressions of Catalan Gothic. It was built on the proceeds of Barcelona's maritime supremacy in the Middle Ages.

The Ribera Literally 'The Seaside' or 'waterfront', the Ribera was the city's centre of gravity in the 13th century, when Catalan commerce dominated the Western Mediterranean ports. Successful merchants and entrepreneurs set themselves up in fine town houses close to the busy shore, cheek by jowl with labourers, dock porters and craftsmen. The street names of the Ribera still reflect the trades once practised here: Assaonadors (tanners), Espaseria (swordmaking), Argenteria (silversmithing), Sombreres (hatters).

People's Church Santa Maria was begun in 1329, the foundation stone commemorating the Catalan conquest of Sardinia. Sometimes referred to as the Cathedral of the Ribera, Santa Maria has always been a popular church, the focus of this once busy harbour district; the whole population is supposed to have toiled on its construction for 50 years. The life of the Ribera was reflected in decorative touches such as delightful depictions of dock-workers on doors and the altar. The altar is crowned by a sculpture of a 15th-century ship. Other than that, the interior of the church is almost bare; its elaborate baroque furnishings were torched during the Civil War, and now the calm and symmetry created by its high vaults and by the majestic spacing of its octagonal columns can be appreciated without distraction.

HIGHLIGHTS

Santa Maria
● Rose window in west front

In the Ribera
● Passeig del Born with central Rambla
● 19th-century glass and iron Born Market building
● Fosser de les Moreres plaza
● Medieval houses in Carrer de les Caputxes

INFORMATION

✚ H9
✉ Plaça de Santa Maria
☎ 93 310 23 90
🕐 Daily 9:30–1:30, 4:30–8
Ⓜ Jaume 1
🚌 14, 17, 36, 39, 45, 51, 57, 59, 64
♿ Good
🎫 Free
↔ Museu Picasso (➤ 42)

The magnificent interior of Santa Maria del Mar

PORT VELL

Renovations in the early 1990s reclaimed the Old Port and reintegrated it into city life. The modern Rambla de Mar walk way extends acoss the water to the Maremagnum complex, a development of shops, restaurants, entertainment and an aquarium, at the heart of the Old Port.

HIGHLIGHTS

- Ascent of Columbus Column
- Harbour trip on one of the Golondrine pleasure boats
- 19th-century timber-clad submarine *Ictineo*

INFORMATION

Aquarium

- ➕ H10
- ✉ Moll d'Espanya
- ☎ 93 221 74 74
- ⏱ Jul–Aug: Mon–Fri 9:30AM–11PM (weekends 9:30AM –9:30PM). Jun and Sep: daily 9:30AM–9:30PM. Oct–May: daily 9:30AM–9PM
- 🍴 Café
- Ⓜ Drassanes
- 🚌 14, 17, 36, 38, 40, 45, 57, 59, 64, 91
- ♿ None
- 💰 Moderate
- ↔ Drassanes (➤ 36)

Monument a Colom

- ➕ G9
- ✉ Plaça del Portal de la Pau
- ☎ 93 302 52 24
- ⏱ Jun–Sep: daily 9–9. Apr–May: Tue–Sat 10–2, 3:30–8; Sun and hols 10–8. Oct–Mar: Tue–Sat 10–2, 3:30–7; Sun and hols 10–7
- Ⓜ Barceloneta, Drassanes
- 🚌 19, 40 to Port Vell, or 14, 17, 36, 38, 40, 45, 57, 59, 64, 91
- ♿ Good
- 💰 Expensive
- ↔ Drassanes (➤ 36), Palau de Mar (➤ 45)

Back to the sea Barcelona has often been accused of ignoring the sea on which so much of its prosperity depended. In the past, the closest most tourists came to it was an ascent of the 51m Monument a Colom, at the seaward end of the Rambla, which commemorates the return of Columbus from the New World in 1493. The port area remained unvisited. Now, the Port Vell is given over to pleasure and most commercial activity takes place among the modern port installations to the west, although the big ferries to the Balearics still depart from here.

Peninsula The Maremagnum, a huge covered shopping and entertainment complex, is connected to the mainland by the Rambla de Mar. This obelisk-lined walkway is usually thronged with tourists but there are peaceful spots for a stroll. It's particularly appealing in summer, when you want a sea breeze, and at night, when a couple of the clubs and bars are worth checking out. Apart from the Maremagnum's clutch of uninspiring shops and restaurants, you'll find the aquarium, which is one of the largest in Europe and requires a good couple of hours for a visit. Don't miss walking through the 80m long glass tunnel – sharks are just a few centimetres away from your face. Also worthwhile is the IMAX cinema, which screens spectacular natural history and other films.

PALAU DE MAR

Dispel any ignorance of Catalonia's past with a visit to the entertaining Palace of the Sea, home to the Museum of Catalan History. Innovative exhibits clarify what has gone into the creation of this nation within a nation.

Catalonia! Catalonia! An imposing late 19th-century warehouse, which has been expensively converted into offices and restaurants, houses the stimulating Museu d'Història de Catalunya. Although Catalan history may be something of a closed book to casual visitors, it's worth knowing more about – the past speaks volumes about the present and current aspirations. General Franco wanted Catalan identity to disappear altogether; the museum is one of many initiatives that the regional government (the Generalitat) took to restore it. The exhibits are exclusively in Catalan but many are self-explanatory, and Spanish and English summaries are available.

Intriguing exhibits   The quayside museum highlights themes from history in a series of spaces grouped around a central atrium. There are few artefacts on display, but exhibits are truly ingenious; you can work an Arab waterwheel, walk over a skeleton in its shallow grave, climb on to a cavalier's charger and test the weight of his armour, enter a medieval forest, peer into a primitive stone cabin, enjoy a driver's-eye view from an early tram, and cower in a Civil War air-raid shelter. Sound effects, films and interactive screens enhance the experience.

HIGHLIGHTS

- Early ship packed with amphorae
- Moorish shop
- Sinister Civil Guards pursuing insurgents
- Civil War machine-gun emplacement
- Franco era schoolroom
- 1930s kitchen with objects to handle
- First edition of George Orwell's *Homage to Catalonia*
- 1960s tourist bar with Speak Inglis/Parle Frances sign

Bronze exhibit from this innovative museum

INFORMATION

- ✚ H9/10
- ✉ Plaça de Pau Vila 3
- ☎ 93 225 47 00/26/32
- 🕐 Tue–Thu 10–7; Fri–Sat 10–8; Sun and hols 10–2:30
- 🍴 Café
- Ⓜ Barceloneta
- 🚌 14, 17, 39, 40, 45, 57, 59, 64
- ♿ Good
- 💰 Moderate
- ↔ Barceloneta (► 48), Port Vell (► 44)

23

PARC DE LA CIUTADELLA

HIGHLIGHTS

- Hivernacle conservatory
- Umbracle conservatory

Sculptures
- *Sorrow* by Josep Llimona
- *Lady with Parasol* by Joan Roig, 1884 (in Zoo)
- Modern *Homage to the Universal Exposition of 1888*
- *Homage to Picasso* by A Tàpies (1983) (on Passeig de Picasso)

INFORMATION

- J9
- Arc de Triomf, Barcelona
- 14, 39, 40, 41, 42, 51, 141
- Barceloneta (► 48), Museu Picasso (► 42), Santa Maria del Mar (► 43)

In the 1860s and 1870s the great Citadel, a longtime symbol of Bourbon oppression, was gleefully demolished. In its place the city laid out its first public park, still a shady haven on the edge of the city centre.

The Citadel Covering an area almost as big as the city itself at the time, the monstrous Citadel was built to cow the Catalans after their defeat on 11 September 1714 by the new Bourbon monarch of Spain, Philip V. (Paradoxically, this date has become Catalonia's national holiday). A garrison of 8,000 troops kept the population in check, and the Citadel was loathed as a place where local patriots were executed. In 1868, the Catalan General Juan Prim y Prats came to power and ensured his popularity by ordering its demolition, a process already begun by the enthusiastic citizenry.

The park today The public park that took the Citadel's place (and name) shows little trace of the great fortress, though the Arsenal now houses the Catalan Parliament and the Museum of Modern Art (► 47). Other structures are leftovers from the Universal Expo of 1888: an ornate Arc de Triomf (Triumphal Arch), and a *modernista* café designed by Domènech i Montaner and now home to the Zoological Museum. The zoo itself is to the south (► 59). Throughout the park, fine trees and shrubs and a boating lake soften the formal layout. The imposing Font Monumental, an extraordinary fountain feature, incorporates just about every allegorical element possible beneath its own triumphal arch – Niagara Falls meets the Brandenburg Gate. Some of the extravagant iron- and rock-work is attributed to the young Antoni Gaudí.

MUSEU D'ART MODERN

The remoteness of Barcelona's Museum of Modern Art, on the far side of the Parc de la Ciutadella, seems to isolate its treasures. But the opportunity to view so many examples of that extraordinary effusion of artistic creativity known as Catalan Modernisme, makes the trip across the park more than worthwhile.

Hidden talents The *modernista* architects of Catalonia are well enough known, but their artist contemporaries have remained relatively obscure. The collection on display here, the most comprehensive in the world, definitively illuminates their work; nowhere else will you see such a splendid array of the works of these decorative artists, whose originality and craftsmanship matched the talent of the architects with whom they collaborated. The collection spans from the 1860s into the 1930s.

Arts and crafts Somewhat incongruously, the collection is housed in part of the Catalan Government building, the old Arsenal. After you have absorbed the exotic African scenes of Marià Fortuny (1838–94), look out for the work of Ramon Casas (1866–1932) and Santiago Rusinyol (1861–1931), long-standing friends and frequenters of the El Quatre Gats bar and restaurant. But even they are upstaged by the opulence of the decorative arts displays, an outstanding array of furniture, jewellery, textiles, sculpture, ceramics and painted screens. *Modernisme* was succeeded by a movement known as *Noucentisme*, an attempt to reintroduce the more harmonious values of classical and Mediterranean art. Be sure to look for paintings by Joaquim Sunyer (1874–1956) and sculpture by Enric Casanovas (1882–1948).

HIGHLIGHTS

- Casas, *Corpus Christi Procession* (c1898)
- Casas, original of *Quatre Cats* tandem picture (1897)
- Rusinyol, *Montmartre* paintings
- Joaquim Mir, landscapes
- Gaudí, iron gates from Casa Vicens (1883–5)
- Gaspar Homar, bed and other furniture (c1904)
- Joan Busquets, oratory from Casa Cendoya
- Sunyer, *Portrait of Maria Llimona de Carles* (1917)
- Gargallo, *Head of Picasso* (1917)
- Gargallo, *Gran Ballerina* (1929)

INFORMATION

- ✚ J9
- ✉ Plaça d'Armes, Parc de la Ciutadella
- ☎ 93 319 57 28
- 🕐 Tue–Sat 10–7; Sun and hols 10–2:30
- 🚇 Arc de Triomf, Barceloneta
- 🚌 14, 17, 36, 39, 40, 41, 42, 51, 57, 59, 64, 141
- ♿ Good
- 💵 Inexpensive
- ↔ Parc de la Ciutadella (➤ 46)
- ❓ Shop

47

BARCELONETA & PORT OLÍMPIC

HIGHLIGHTS

- Original Barceloneta house, Sant Carles 6
- Plaça de la Barceloneta with baroque Church of Sant Miquel
- Beach sculpture *Homage to Barceloneta* by Rebecca Horn
- 44m *modernista* water-tower, centrepiece of nearby Parc de la Barceloneta
- Frank Gehry fish sculpture atop Planet Hollywood
- *David and Goliath* sculpture in centre of Ronda Litoral expressway

INFORMATION

- H/J/K10
- Barceloneta, Ciutadella/Vila Olímpica
- Barceloneta 17, 39, 45, 57, 59, 64, 157; Port Olímpic 10, 45, 59, 71, 92
- Port Vell (➤ 44), Parc de la Ciutadella (➤ 46)

Outdoor café in the shadow of Port Olímpic

The streets of Barceloneta, cramped and flagged by flapping laundry, evoke the culture of a traditional Mediterranean seaport. It makes a dramatic contrast to the marina, promenades and glittering buildings of the nearby Port Olímpic, developed as a setting for the 1992 Olympic watersports competitions.

Little Barcelona In the 1750s a military engineer laid out this severe gridded neighbourhood of streets lined with simple two-storey houses, which became an urban village of fisherfolk and harbourmen. Although cut off from the city by railway lines, an expressway and industrial development, the area of Barceloneta neverthe-less acquired a reputation among food lovers. Shacks on the grubby beach served superlative fresh seafood. The late 1980s and 1990s brought an end to this trencherman's shantytown, much to the regret of its innumerable patrons, as the city smartened up its seafront in preparation for the Olympics. By way of compensation, the beach was much improved: Barcelona now has several kilometres of relatively clean seashore (➤ 60).

Olympic outcomes A promenade, the Passeig Marítim, leads north from Barceloneta towards the landmark Mapfre tower skyscraper and its twin, the tallest buildings in Spain. At their foot is a development of cafés and shops fronting the marina of the Port Olímpic and to the north are more new beaches. Inland, along the Ronda Litoral expressway, which skirts the city and links Barceloneta to the Old Town, are green spaces created for the people who now occupy the former Olympic Village apartments.

BARCELONA's
best

Galleries & Museums	*50–51*
Modernista & Modern Architecture	*52–53*
Parks & Gardens	*54–55*
Plaças	*56*
Churches	*57*
Sports & Amusements	*58*
Attractions for Children	*59*
What's Free	*60*

GALLERIES & MUSEUMS

The Cloud and Chair *sculpture outside the Fundació Antoni Tàpies*

The *Ictíneo I*

This venerable ancestor of the Science Museum's submarine *Barcelona* can be seen at the quayside in the Port Vell. Designed by the Catalan patriot and socialist inventor Narcis Monturio, the fish-shaped vessel was built in Barcelona's Nuevo Vulcano shipyard and launched in 1859. It proved supremely seaworthy despite the fact that it was driven solely by human muscle-power. Government indifference kept Spain from exploiting this surprising lead in submarine navigation.

See Top 25 Sights for
CENTRE DE CULTURA CONTEMPORÀNEA (➤ 34)
COLLECIÓ THYSSEN–BORNEMISZA (MUSEU MONESTIR DE PEDRALBES) (➤ 25)
FUNDACIÓ JOAN MIRÓ (➤ 31)
MUSEU D'ART CONTEMPORANI (➤ 34)
MUSEU D'ART MODERN (➤ 47)
MUSEU DE LES ARTS DECORATIVES AND MUSEU DE CERÀMICA (PALAU DE PEDRALBES) (➤ 24)
MUSEU D'HISTÒRIA DE CATALUNYA (PALAU DE MAR) (➤ 45)
MUSEU D'HISTÒRIA DE LA CIUTAT (➤ 40)
MUSEU MONESTIR DE PEDRALBES (➤ 25)
MUSEU MARÍTIM (➤ 36)
MUSEU NACIONAL D'ART DE CATALUNYA (➤ 30)
MUSEU PICASSO (➤ 42)

FUNDACIÓ ANTONI TÀPIES

Nowadays, Joan Miró's mantle as the Grand Old Man of Catalan art is convincingly worn by Tàpies, whose earthy creations can be seen in this magnificently converted *modernista* building by Domènech i Montaner. The building announces its purpose with Tàpies' roof-top sculpture *Cloud and Chair*, an extraordinary extrusion of wire and tubing.

✚ H7　✉ Carrer d'Aragó 255　☎ 93 487 03 15　🕐 Tue–Sun 11–8　🚇 Passeig de Gràcia　♿ Good　💷 Moderate

MUSEU DE LA CIENCIA I DE LA TÈCNICA

Housed in a splendid *modernista* building at the foot of the Tibidabo heights, this up-to-date Museum of Science and Technology is the finest of its kind in Spain. Many of its exhibits and displays encourage participation, and it is a great favourite with children, who have exclusive use of some of the facilities. There is an Optics Room, a Computer Room, a Planetarium and a Foucault Pendulum. Perched outside is the museum's emblem, the submarine *Barcelona*.

🔳 G2 ✉ Teodor Roviralta 55 ☎ 93 212 60 50 🕐 Tue–Sun 10–8 🍴 Café 🚇 Tibidabo, then Tramvia Blau ♿ Good 💶 Moderate

MUSEU FREDERIC MARÈS

There are three main reasons for visiting this museum named after the long-lived sculptor and obsessive collector Frederic Marès: its setting overlooking the courtyard garden of the Royal Palace; its inexhaustible collection of sculpture from pre-Roman times to the 19th century; and last (but far from least), the section known as the Collecció Sentimental (Sentimental Museum), with its surreal array of everyday objects from the 15th to the 19th centuries.

🔳 H9 ✉ Plaça St Iu 5 ☎ 93 310 58 00 🕐 Tue–Sat 10–5; Sun and hols 10–2 🍴 Café 🚇 Jaume I ♿ Few 💶 Moderate

MUSEU DEL PERFUM

How appropriate that a scent museum should be situated among the sleek shops and expensive boutiques of the prestigious Passeig de Gràcia. The 5,000-item collection ranges from the time of the Pharoahs to today; there is even a perfume bottle designed by Dalí.

🔳 I17 ✉ Passeig de Gràcia 39 ☎ 93 216 01 46 🕐 Mon–Fri 10:30–2, 4:30–8; Sat 10:30–2. Closed hols 🚇 Passeig de Gràcia ♿ Few 💶 Free

MUSEU TÈXTIL I D'INDUMENTÀRIA

The very existence of the Museum of Textiles and Fashion is a reminder that Barcelona rode to prosperity in the 1800s on the back of the textile industry. The collection's range extends far beyond 19th-century Catalonia; there are costumes of all kinds, from the Middle Ages to more or less contemporary times – witness the inventive creations of Balenciaga. A bonus is the brace of medieval palaces that house the collection.

🔳 H9 ✉ Montcada 12 ☎ 93 310 45 16/319 76 03 🕐 Tue–Sat 10–8; Sun and hols 10–3 🍴 Café-restaurant 🚇 Jaume I ♿ Few 💶 Inexpensive

Treasures of the Marès

The sheer number of exhibits in the sculpture section of the Marès Museum is almost overwhelming; look for the printed sheets (in English) that point out star pieces like the 12th-century *St Peter* from San Pedro de Roda and the 12th–13th-century *Madonna and Child* from Plandogau. Upstairs, in the section known as the Sentimental Museum, you are certain to be amazed by the endless cases of fans, pipes, playing cards and buttons.

Exhibit from the Museu Frederic Marès

51

MODERNISTA & MODERN ARCHITECTURE

Catalan creation

The late 19th-century *modernista* movement embraced a contemporary interest in the decorative arts – buildings were ornamented with extraordinary detail, both inside and out. *Modernista* proponents believed that interior decoration and furniture were as important to a building as its façade. This 'total art' concept infiltrated all areas of Barcelona; although the Eixample has a high concentration of *Modernista* architecture, there are traces all across the city – in doorways, on paving patterns, railings, lamp posts, and even shop interiors.

The façade of the Casa Fuster

See Top 25 Sights for
CASA MILÀ (➤ 32)
MANZANA DE LA DISCÒRDIA (➤ 33)
PALAU DE LA MÚSICA CATALANA (➤ 38)
PARC GÜELL (➤ 27)
SAGRADA FAMILIA (➤ 37)

CASA COMALAT
Many *modernista* architects gave their buildings an elaborate street façade, leaving the rear to look after itself. Salvador Valeri's Casa Comalat of 1911 is an exception, with gloriously over-the-top ornamentation on both frontages.
➕ H6 ✉ Diagonal 442/Corsega 316 🚇 Diagonal

CASA FUSTER
This corner building of 1910 on Passeig de Gràcia is one of Domènech i Montaner's last urban edifices, with a playful yet masterly combination of classical and neo-Gothic styles and motifs.
➕ H6 ✉ Gran de Gràcia 2–4/Passeig de Gràcia 132 🚇 Diagonal
🚌 22, 24, 28, 39

CASA MACAYA
Barcelona's medieval palaces served as models for Puig i Cadafalch's 1901 building, now a culture centre. It gives you a chance to explore the interior of one of the more sumptuous creations of Catalan *Modernisme*.
➕ J6 🏛 Centre Cultural de la Fundació La Caixa, Passeig de Sant Joan 108 ☎ 93 458 89 07 🕐 Tue–Sat 11–8; Sun and hols 11–3
🍽 Café 🚇 Verdaguer 💰 Inexpensive

CASA TERRADES
Puig i Cadafalch's huge 1905 building, known also as the Casa de les Punxes (House of Spikes), occupies the whole of an island site in the Eixample. Its profusion of towers and gables would seem to make it more at home in Bavaria than on the Mediterranean.
➕ H6 ✉ Diagonal 416–420 🚇 Diagonal

CASA VICENS
Gaudí's first major commission (1878), this summer residence in Gràcia is generally reckoned to have paved the way for *Modernisme*, less with its neo-Arabic decoration than with its structure and layout.
➕ H5 ✉ Carrer de les Carolines 18–24 🚇 Fontana 🚌 22, 24, 28, 39

HOSPITAL DE LA SANTA CREU I SANT PAU
Disliking the monotony of the Eixample, Domènech i Montaner deliberately defied it by aligning the buildings of Barcelona's first modern hospital at 45 degrees to its grid of streets. The hospital was laid out

like a self-contained village with patients housed in 48 separate pavilions; a profusion of decoration was intended to speed healing.

✚ K6 ✉ Sant Antoni Maria Claret 167 🚇 Hospital de Sant Pau

The striking edifice of the Hospital de Sant Pau

MIES VAN DER ROHE GERMANY PAVILION

Germany's contribution to the Expo of 1929 was this supremely cool construction of steel, glass and marble that reinvented all the rules of architecture. It has become an icon of modern (as opposed to *modernista*) design. Yet amazingly, the building was demolished when the fair was over. It was rebuilt by devoted admirers in the mid-1980s and is now a compulsory stop for visiting international architecture students.

✚ E8 ✉ Pavelló Barcelona, Avinguda del Marquès de Comillas
☎ 93 423 40 16 🕐 Daily 10–8 🚇 Espanya 🎫 Inexpensive

PALAU GÜELL

Gaudí's first mature work was this magnificent palace for his patron Eusebi Güell, begun in 1886 when the architect was aged 34. Painstakingly designed and constructed from the finest materials available at the time, it's a masterpiece. The paradoxical effect of simplicity and space amid all the innovation and finery is striking. The rooftop terrace, with chimneys decorated with glazed tiling, prefigures the work on the Casa Milà and is a particular delight.

✚ G9 ✉ Carrer Nou de la Rambla 3–5 ☎ 93 317 39 74
🕐 Mon–Fri 10–2, 4–7:30. Closed Sat and Sun 🚇 Liceu

Relics of an era

Modernista architecture was embraced by the Universal Exhibition of 1888 and was at its peak for the 20 years following the event. Many of the buildings from this time no longer exist but Domènech i Montaner's exhibition restaurant, Castell dels Tres Dragons (the Castle of the Three Dragons), has survived. This jolly neo-medieval brick and iron building was subsequently used by the architect as his studio and today houses the city's Zoological Museum.

PARKS & GARDENS

See Top 25 Sights for
MONTJUÏC (► 28)
PALAU DE PEDRALBES GARDENS (► 24)
PARC DE LA CIUTADELLA (► 46)
PARC GÜELL (► 27)

Projects not plans

In the early 1980s, the City Council of Barcelona decided to encourage small-scale civic projects like parks and plazas rather than grandiose schemes. The results can be seen all over the city, where new paving, trees and sculpture embellish the urban scene – and help to consolidate Barcelona's international reputation as a centre of exciting and progressive design.

PARC DEL CLOT

This ingenious neighbourhood park in the eastern suburbs incorporates the walls of the old railway yards it replaced. Among the features are a plaza, overhead walkways, enigmatic sculptures and artificial hills.

➕ L7 ⊠ Escultors Claperós ⏰ May–Aug: daily 10–9. Apr–Sep: daily 10–8. Mar, Oct: daily 10–7. Nov–Feb: daily 10–6 🚇 Glories ♿ Free

PARC DE LA CREUETA DEL COLL

Serving the densely inhabited suburb of Vallcarca, this new park is spectacularly sited among the cliff-faces of an old quarry. The lake and artificial beach are hugely popular in summer.

➕ J3 ⊠ Mar de Déu del Coll ⏰ May–Aug: daily 10–9. Apr, Sep daily 10–8. Mar, Oct: daily 10–7. Nov–Feb: daily 10–6 🚌 25,28,87 ♿ Free

PARC DE L'ESPANYA INDUSTRIAL

The post-modern design of Europe's oddest municipal park flies in the face of all the rules in the landscape architect's book. Trees are almost outnumbered by the giant lighthouses lined up along one side of the site; one plane tree grows out of a heap of rocks; and the Mediterranean sun beats down mercilessly on the blinding white stairways. But children love the monster metal slide, which is styled to look like St George and the Dragon, and there are always plenty of customers for the boats on the lake.

➕ E6/7 ⊠ Cicero ⏰ Open access 🚇 Sants-Estació

PARC DEL FOSSAR DE LA PEDRERA

This new commemorative park was laid out in a quarry next to the splendid Cementiri del Sud Oest, which is notable for its extravagant *modernista* family tombs. Many of those on the losing side in the Civil War were buried here, including the president of Catalonia, Lluís Companys. His tomb is the modest, minimalist centrepiece of the park.

➕ C9 🚌 9, 38, 72, 109

PARC DEL LABERINT D'HORTA

Lovingly restored, this 18th-century retreat is on the wooded slopes of Vall d'Hebron high above the built-up area of Barcelona. One delight succeeds another as you explore steps and pathways leading from the neo-Arab mansion (once the focal point of the estate that was the basis for the park) to the

great pool at the top of the garden. There are fountains, canals, sculptures and a gorge with a mock cemetery and hermit's hut. At the heart of the extensive garden is the eponymous Labyrinth, a beautifully hedged maze with a statue of Eros at its centre.

🔲 L1 ✉ Passeig dels Castanyers 🕐 May–Aug: daily 10–9. Mar, Apr, Sep, Oct: daily 10–8. Nov–Feb: daily 10–6 🚌 10, 27, 60, 73, 76, 85 🚫 None 💶 Inexpensive

PARC JOAN MIRÓ
The sculptor's giant brightly coloured *Woman and Bird* dominates this park with its orderly rows of palm trees. It is also known as the Parc de l'Escorxador.

🔲 E7 ✉ Tarragona 🕐 Open access 🚇 Tarragona, Espanya

PLAÇA DELS PAÏSOS CATALANS
Basically a concrete canopy laid out on ground once occupied by railway tracks, this open space is more sculpture show than park: Shining steel canopies take the place of trees.

🔲 E6 🕐 Open access 🚇 Sants-Estació

The rather bizarre and futuristic Parc de l'Espanya Industrial

Trees in the city
The natural vegetation of Barcelona is the evergreen oak. The noble plane trees that line so many streets, including the Rambla, were introduced into Spain some 600 years ago. New plantings favour the Italian cypress, a symbol of hospitality, and the date palm, brought back from the Spanish colonies a century or so ago.

55

PLAÇAS

See Top 25 Sights for
PLAÇA DEL REI (► 40)
PLAÇA SANT JAUME (► 41)

The very hub of cosmopolitan Barcelona – the Plaça de Catalunya

PLAÇA DE CATALUNYA
City life and public transport routes seem to converge on this spacious central square, not least because of its position at the upper end of the Rambla. The main landmark is the huge slab-like Corte Inglès department store; the population of monuments and statues is considerable. A 1991 addition commemorates the popular pre-Civil War politician Francesc Macià.
🏛 H8 🚇 Catalunya

PLAÇA REIAL
With its arcades and classical façades, this grandiose and splendidly symmetrical square is in complete contrast to the crooked streets and alleyways of the surrounding Barri Gòtic. Built in the mid-19th century on the model of the squares of Paris, it is a favourite hangout of idlers and winos, though it is considerably smarter than it once was. The elaborate lamp posts by Antoni Gaudí are as impressive as the tall palm trees.
🏛 G9 🚇 Liceu

PLAÇA DEL SOL
This neat little square is a nice enough place for a coffee while wandering the streets of Gràcia by day, but it really comes into its own after dark, particularly at weekends. Café del Sol, with its cool *terraza* and El Dorado are well worth checking out before heading off to a club.
🏛 H5 🚇 Fontana

PLAÇA RIUS I TAULET
Antoni Rovira i Trias, whose adventurous plan for the Eixample was rejected in favour of Ildefons Cerdà's grid plan back in 1859, designed the magnificent 30m bell tower that dominates this pleasant Gràcia square. Quiet during the day, it becomes much livelier at night and it's one of the centres of activity during Gràcia's annual *Festa Major* (► 26).
🏛 H6 🚇 Fontana

Plaça de Catalunya in the Civil War

In the military uprising that signalled the start of the Civil War, the rebels' attempt to storm the telephone exchange on the eastern corner of the square was repelled by armed workers. Later, in the confused fighting between the rival parties of the Left, the Anarchists held the Raval district to the west, while the Communists commanded the square with a machine-gun mounted in the 'O' of the rooftop sign of the old Hotel Colón.

CHURCHES

See Top 25 Sights for
CATEDRAL (➤ 39)
MUSEU MONESTIR DE PEDRALBES (➤ 25)
SAGRADA FAMILIA (➤ 37)
SANTA MARIA DEL MAR (➤ 43)

BETLEM
The Bethlehem Church, a landmark on the Rambla, was formed as a Jesuit foundation in 1681. As such, it aroused the particular fury of anti-clerical mobs in 1936, when its interior was torched and destroyed. The splendidly ornate porch remains.
➕ G8 ✉ Rambla 107/Carme 2 🚇 Liceu

DE LA MERCÉ
Together with St Eulàlia, Our Lady of Mercy is one of Barcelona's patron saints. Her church, one of the finest baroque buildings in the city, was erected in the 1760s, replacing a much earlier building.
➕ H9 ✉ Plaça de la Mercé 🚇 Drassanes

SANTA MARIA DEL PI
The focal point of a trio of tiny squares, the monumentally plain exterior of this Barri Gòtic church conceals an equally austere interior, a single nave in characteristic Catalan Gothic style. The main façade, its statues long since gone, has a fine rose window. The octagonal bell tower is 54m high.
➕ G9 🕐 Weekdays 8:30–1, 4:30–9, otherwise 8–2, 5–9 🚇 Liceu

SANT MIQUEL DEL PORT
This fine mid-18th century baroque building faces the square named after it in the centre of Barceloneta.
➕ H10 ✉ Plaça de la Barceloneta 🚇 Barceloneta

SANT PAU DEL CAMP
It is a surprise to find a village church named St Paul-in-the-Fields so close to the old city centre, but the Romanesque structure really was in the middle of the countryside when it was built at the beginning of the 12th century. It replaced an even older building, probably dating from Visigothic times, which was wrecked by Moorish invaders; some of the material from this original building was used to construct the columns. The façade's wonderfully simple and severe sculptural decoration includes the symbols of the Evangelists and the Hand of God.
➕ G9 ✉ Sant Pau 101 🕐 Mon, Wed–Sun 11–1 🚇 Paral.lel

Tragic Week
The outbreak of the Civil War in 1936 saw the destruction of church interiors in Barcelona, but the Setmana Tragica (Tragic Week) of July 1909 was even worse; more than 80 religious buildings were burnt and rioters danced in the streets with the disinterred bodies of priests and nuns.

Rose window inside Santa Maria del Pi

SPORTS & AMUSEMENTS

Catch a ride at Montjuïc

Out of town

City dwellers though they may be, *Barcelonins* love the great outdoors. The Costa Daurada and Costa Brava are as popular with locals as they are with northern Europeans. Just behind the great city rises the Sierra de Collserola, with its forests and footpaths. The Pyrenees, two hours' drive away, have long been the preserve of Catalan climbing clubs.

See Top 25 Sights for
ANELLA OLÍMPICA (MONTJUÏC) (► 28)

ESTADI OLÍMPIC

The Barcelona Dragons play against other teams in the American Football World League on Sundays, April–June. Buy tickets on the day at the stadium.
⊞ E9 ⊠ Avinguda de l'Estadi ☎ 93 425 49 49 🚌 61

GALERIA OLÍMPICA

The video displays and souvenir showcases of this Olympic Gallery recall some of the glories of the Olympic fortnight in 1992.
⊞ E9 ⊠ South Gate, Estadi Olimpic ☎ 93 426 06 60 🕐 Jul–Aug: Mon–Sat 10–2, 4–8; Sun and hols 10–2. Sep: Mon–Fri 10–2, 4–8; hols 10–2; weekends closed. Apr–Jun: Mon–Sat 10–2, 4–7; Sun and hols 10–2. Oct–Mar: Mon–Fri 10–1, 4–6; hols 10–2; weekends closed
🚌 61 🎫 Inexpensive

NOU CAMP

The suppression of Catalan self-respect under the Franco regime made Barcelona football club (FC Barcelona) a potent symbol of identity. The passion 'Barça' attracted then, particularly when pitted against rival Real Madrid, has not diminished despite today's more enlightened political climate. The 98,000-seat Nou Camp stadium is the home of the club and a great shrine of world soccer. If you want to go to a match, book early; most seats will be already taken by the club's 100,000-plus members. The museum under the terraces has an array of trophies and replays of magic moments in the club's history.
Museo del Futbol Club Barcelona: ⊞ D5 ⊠ Aristides Maillol ☎ 93 496 36 00 🕐 Mon–Sat 10–6:30, Sun and hols 10–2 🚇 Collblanc, Maria Cristina ♿ Good 🎫 Moderate

PARC D'ATRACCIONS DE MONTJUÏC

The Montjuïc amusement park, with its 40-odd rides, has everything you would expect plus a superb site on the slopes of the mountain overlooking the city and the harbour.
⊞ F9 ⊠ Carretera de Montjuïc ☎ 93 441 70 24/93 442 31 75 🚇 Paral.lel, then Montjuïc funicular, then Teleferique 🎫 Entry inexpensive, rides moderate

VELODROM DE HORTA

Together with Montjuïc and the Olympic Village, the Vall d'Hebron on the lower slopes of the Sierra de Collserola was one of the three sites of the 1992 Olympics. The elliptical Velodrome was built to seat 14,000 for the 1984 World Cycling Championships.
⊞ L1 ⊠ Passeig de la Vall d'Hebron 🚌 10, 27, 60, 73, 76, 85

ATTRACTIONS FOR CHILDREN

See Top 25 Sights for
AQUARIUM / IMAX CINEMA (PORT VELL) (► 44)
POBLE ESPANYOL (► 29)

GOLONDRINES
Barcelona's swallow-boats (► 19) do harbour trips
from the Port Vell quayside, and to Port Olímpic.
🚩 G10 ☎ 93 442 31 06 ⏰ Closed 15 Dec–1 Jan 💷 Moderate

MUSEU DE CERA
The wax museum in the Rambla is an old favourite,
with exciting special effects. Look out for Superman
on the rooftop.
🚩 G9 ✉ Passeig de la Banca, 7 ☎ 93 317 26 49 ⏰ Jul–Sep:
daily 10–8. Oct–Jun: Mon–Fri 10–1:30, 4–7:30; weekends and hols
11–2, 4:30–8:30 💷 Moderate

PARC DE LA CIUTADELLA
This large park, convenient to the city centre, has
playgrounds, bike and skate rentals, and the Parc
Zoologic. The most popular of the zoo's inhabitants
is Copito de Nieve (Snowflake), the only albino
gorilla in captivity. In the separate children's section
smaller animals can be
touched (► 46).
Zoo: 🚩 J9 ☎ 93 221 04 87
⏰ May–Aug: daily 9:30–7:30. Apr
and Sep: daily 10–7 Oct–Feb: daily
10–5 🚇 Barceloneta, Ciutadella

PARC D'ATRACCIONS
DE TIBIDABO
This popular amusement
park, with wonderful views
from the summit of 542m-
high Tibidabo, has been
modernised and renamed
La Muntanya Màgica (Magic
Mountain). Built on several
levels of the mountaintop,
high-tech attractions sit
alongside traditional
fairground rides – some
features, like the red
monoplane (1922) and the
Haunted Castle (1955),
have entertained children
for years.
🚩 G1 ✉ Plaça Tibidabo 3–4
☎ 93 211 79 42 ⏰ Apr–mid Sep:
daily noon–1AM; Sep–Mar: weekends
and hols noon–7 🚇 Tibidabo (then
Tramvia Blau and funicular)

Transported
Transportation around a new city
always delights children. Unusual
ways of travelling in Barcelona
include the vintage tram, Tramvia
Blau; the funicular up to Tibidabo;
and the funicular and cable-cars
that serve Montjuïc (► 28).

*The Rambla's street
entertainers*

WHAT'S FREE

Rambling along the Carrer del Bisbe in the Barri Gòtic

Walking the streets

Even more than most cities, the best way to experience Barcelona, as well as the cheapest, is on foot. Many streets in the Barri Gòtic are traffic-free, and the compact nature of the old city means that walking is often not only the quickest way to get about, but also the most interesting.

THE BEACH
Barcelona is one of those rare cities with a good bathing beach. The sandy shore extends for more than 4km from Barceloneta northwards, with children's playgrounds, plenty of showers and good access for people with disabilities.

MUSEUMS
Museums run by the City Council allow free entry on the first Sunday of the month: the Picasso Museum (➤ 42), the City History Museum (➤ 40), the Frederic Marès Museum (➤ 51), the Ceramics Museum (➤ 24), Pedralbes Monastery (➤ 25) and the Textile Museum (➤ 51).

PARKS
What a privilege to walk around Gaudí's Parc Güell (➤ 27) – and it doesn't cost a peseta. Alternatively, explore the magnificent greenery embellishing the slopes of Montjuïc or relax by the lake in the Parc de la Ciutadella. Entry is free to all.

POBLE ESPANYOL
You can visit this re-created Spanish Village at no charge after 8PM on Wednesday, Thursday and Sunday (➤ 29).

SARDANA
Circles of dancers perform the complex and carefully controlled steps of Catalonia's national dance at a number of places in the city, including the Cathedral square. Be there at 6:30PM on Saturdays (Feb–Jul and Sep–Nov only) or at noon on Sundays or holidays. Or head for Plaça Sant Jaume (➤ 41) at 6PM on Sundays. Turn up and dance or just watch if it all looks a little complicated.

SCULPTURE
The City Council's vigorous promotion of new parks and plazas included a programme of public sculpture (with the goal of creating focal points in otherwise featureless suburban areas). This programme has few equals among modern cities, and you can come across some startling modern sculpture in the most surprising places. Prominent pieces include works by Joan Miró (Parc Joan Miró ➤ 55), Roy Lichtenstein (Passeig de Colom ➤ 44) and Rebecca Horn (Barceloneta/Port Olímpic ➤ 48).

STREET PERFORMERS
The entertainment along the Rambla is always free, and the human statues, jugglers, street musicians and other talents can be surprisingly good.

BARCELONA
where to...

EAT

Old City 62–63
Eixample & Gràcia 64–65
Barceloneta & Port Olímpic 66
Upper Barcelona 67
Tapas Bars & Cafés 68–69

SHOP

Malls & Department Stores 70
Arts, Crafts & Design 71
Fashion 72–73
Shoes & Accessories 74

Books & Music 75
Food Shops & Markets 76
Gifts & Antiques 77

BE ENTERTAINED

Bars, Discos & Clubs 78–79
Film, Theatre & Music 80–81
Popular Music 82
Traditional Entertainment 83

STAY

Luxury Hotels 84
Mid-Range Hotels 85
Budget Accommodation 86

OLD CITY

Prices

For dinner per person, without drinks, expect to pay approximately:

£   up to 2,500ptas

££   up to 5,000ptas

£££   more than 5,000ptas

Catalan Cooking

Catalonia is generally reckoned to have one of the great regional cuisines of Spain. It is based on good ingredients from the varied countryside and on seafood from the Mediterranean and the Atlantic. Four principal sauces are used. There is *sofregit* (onion, tomato and garlic cooked in olive oil); with added sweet pepper, aubergine and courgette it becomes *samfaina*. *Picada* is made by pounding nuts, fried bread, parsley, saffron and other ingredients in a mortar. Finally there is garlic mayonnaise, *alioli*.

AGUT D'AVIGNON (££)

Tucked away in the heart of the Barri Gòtic and convenient for civil servants and politicians from the nearby Ajuntament and Generalitat, the Agut does an excellent job interpreting traditional Catalan dishes.

✚ G9 ✉ Trinitat 3 ☎ 93 302 60 34 ✪ Closed Christmas Ⓜ Liceu

AMAYA (££)

Deservedly popular Basque restaurant and tapas bar specialising in seafood dishes.

✚ G9 ✉ Rambla 20–24 ☎ 93 302 10 37 Ⓜ Liceu, Drassanes

BRASSERIE FLO (££)

Not far from the Palau de la Música, this brasserie has fine Catalan as well as French cuisine.

✚ H8 ✉ Jonqueres 10 ☎ 93 319 31 02 Ⓜ Urquinaona

CAFÉ DE L'ACADEMIA (££)

Not really a café at all, this restaurant offers some of the best deals in town on a variety of traditional Mediterranean cuisine.

✚ H9 ✉ Lledo 1 ☎ 93 319 82 53 ✪ Closed weekends and hols Ⓜ Jaume I

CA L'ISIDRE (£££)

The sophistication of the seasonal Catalan cooking has enticed King Juan Carlos to brave the distinctly unsophisticated surroundings to dine here when he is in Barcelona.

✚ F9 ✉ Les Flors 12 (Poble Sec) ☎ 93 441 11 39

✪ Closed Sun and hols 🚇 Paral.lel (best by taxi)

CAN CULLERETES (££)

Founded in 1786, Can Culleretes is one of the oldest restaurants in Barcelona. The menu is like a catalogue of old-fashioned Catalan cuisine, but there are modern dishes too. Sample the famous *botifarra* (pork sausage) with its traditional accompaniment of white beans.

✚ G9 ✉ Quintana 5 ☎ 93 317 64 85 ✪ Closed Sun evening, Mon and 21 Jul Ⓜ Liceu

LOS CARACOLES (££)

Succulent chickens roasting on a street-corner spit, scullions scurrying among the devilish din and roaring flames of a medieval kitchen all help to make the 'Snails' unmissably atmospheric.

✚ G9 ✉ Escudellers 14 ☎ 93 302 31 85 Ⓜ Liceu, Drassanes

CASA LEOPOLDO (£££)

Seafood and other fresh ingredients from the nearby Boqueria market have helped make the reputation of this excellent Catalan restaurant.

✚ G8 ✉ Sant Rafael 24 ☎ 93 441 30 14 ✪ Closed Mon and hols Ⓜ Liceu

COMPOSTELA (££)

Just off the Rambles, this convenient restaurant serves Galician specialities in addition to a range of conventional Catalan and other regional Spanish dishes.

H9 ✉ de Ferran 30 ☎ 93 318 23 17 🕐 Closed Tue and Aug 🚇 Jaume I

LA DENTELLIERE (££)

In this intimate French restaurant, crepes, with a multitude of fillings, are the house speciality, although the *pato* (duck) is also superb. Set menus at lunchtime and at night.

H9 ✉ Carrer Ample 26 ☎ 93 319 68 21 🚇 Drassanes

LA FLAUTA MÁGICA (£)

Imaginative vegetarian meals are the hallmark of this popular restaurant but there are also meat dishes on the menu. Book ahead, particularly for weekends

H9 ✉ Banys Vells 18 ☎ 93 268 46 94 🕐 Evenings only 🚇 Liceu

LA FONDA (£)

Brisk, efficient service and great value Catalan cooking mean constant queues outside this three storey restaurant

G9 ✉ Escudellers 10 ☎ 93 301 75 15 🕐 Closed Mon 🚇 Drassanes, Liceu

EL GRAN CAFÉ (££)

This dignified old town instiution dates from the early years of the century.

G9 ✉ Avinyó 9 ☎ 93 318 79 86 🕐 Closed Sun 🚇 Liceu

HOFMAN (£££)

The inventive Mediterranean menu changes every three months and there's an extensive wine list. Friendly and efficient, Hofman is one of the best restaurants in the old town.

H9 ✉ Argenteria 74–78 ☎ 93 319 58 59 🚇 Jaume I

PORTO MAR (£)

In Brazilian cooking, meat is the star, but this place also serves good fresh fish and novel salads. The house *mojito*, (a rum and mint cocktail) is excellent

H9 ✉ Josep Anselm Clave 19 ☎ 93 301 82 27 🚇 Drassanes

LES QUINZE NITS (£)

This comfortable, reliable restaurant has an enviable location beneath the arcades of the elegant Plaça Reial.

G9 ✉ Plaça Reial 6 ☎ 93 317 30 75 🚇 Liceu

QUO VADIS (£££)

A discriminating clientele enjoy well-studied and elegant dishes from Catalonia and other regions of Spain.

G8 ✉ Carme 7 ☎ 93 317 74 47 🕐 Closed Sun 🚇 Liceu

RÍAS DE GALICIA (££)

Daily deliveries of fresh shellfish from Galicia please the crowds who flock here from the nearby exhibition grounds.

E8 ✉ Lleida 7 ☎ 93 424 81 52/93 423 45 70 🚇 Poble Sec, Espanya

LA VERONICA (£)

Excellent pizzas – surprisingly difficult to find in this city – are the mainstays of the menu at this friendly restaurant along with fine salads. In summer, you can dine on the *terraza*.

G9 ✉ Avinyo 30 ☎ 93 412 11 22 🕐 Closed Mon 🚇 Jaume I

Galician Flavors

Many restaurants in Barcelona specialise in Galician cuisine. Galicia, the northwest region of Spain, is famous for its seafood— octopus, crab, scallops, clams and sardines are all simply prepared and delicious. Traditional Galician country fare is also excellent; try *empanadas* (pastry filled with seafood or meat), and *fabada* (bean and sausage stew).

63

EIXAMPLE & GRÀCIA

Special today

Many local people make their midday meal the main one of the day and eat relatively frugally in the evening. One reason for following their example is to benefit from the bargain represented by the *menú del día* (fixed-price menu). It is likely to consist of three or four courses plus bread and a beverage, a combination that would cost considerably more if the dishes were selected individually, particularly in the evening.

BELTXENEA (£££)
Perfectly prepared dishes from the Basque country by Miguel Ezcurra, in luxurious surroundings.
🔶 H7 ✉ Mallorca 275 (Eixample) ☎ 93 215 30 24 🕐 Closed Sat lunch and Sun 🚇 Diagonal, Passeig de Gràcia

BOTAFUMERIO (£££)
This spacious Galician restaurant on Gràcia's main street serves delicious shellfish and a selection of seafood from the country's Atlantic coast.
🔶 H6 ✉ Gran de Gràcia 81 ☎ 93 218 42 30/93 217 96 42 🕐 Closed last 3 weeks Aug 🚇 Fontana

CASA BACH (££)
Tucked away in an anonymous Gràcia *plaça*, this small restaurant is well worth seeking out, particularly for the excellent *menu del día*, which always features one fresh fish dish and home-made desserts.
🔶 H5 ✉ Plaça de la Revolució de Setembre 1868, 15 ☎ 93 213 30 44 🚇 Fontana

CASA LORCA (£)
An Andalusian restaurant in the heart of Gràcia, serving fresh fish and traditional dishes such as *ajoblanco* (cold garlic soup).
🔶 G5 ✉ Esquina (corner) con Carrer Lincoln ☎ 93 415 8194 🚇 Gràcia

CITRUS (££)
Watch the promenaders on Passeig de Gràcia from the window tables of this first-floor restaurant with cool decor, good service and delicious local fare. The pig's trotter stuffed with seafood and wrapped in cabbage leaves is far more tempting than it sounds.
🔶 H7 ✉ Passeig de Gràcia 44 ☎ 93 487 23 45 🚇 Passeig de Gràcia

GARGANTUA Y PANTAGRUEL (££)
Food from the region around Lérida, on a Rabelaisian scale.
🔶 G7 ✉ Aragó 214 ☎ 93 453 20 20 🕐 Closed Sun, Easter, Christmas and Aug 🚇 Passeig de Gràcia

EL GLOP (£)
Convenient to Gràcia, this trendy tavern serves delicious grilled meats.
🔶 J5 ✉ Sant Lluís 24 ☎ 93 213 70 58/ 93 284 83 79 🚇 Joanic

JAUME DE PROVENÇA (£££)
Interesting international dishes vary a menu of Catalan specialities, all prepared with refinement by acclaimed local chef Jaume Bargues.
🔶 F6 ✉ Provença 88 ☎ 93 322 79 31 🕐 Closed Sun evening, Mon, Aug, Christmas and Easter 🚇 Entença

JEAN LUC FIGUERAS (£££)
This elegant restaurant at the bottom end of Gràcia, just off the Diagonal, offers superb Catalan cuisine – and the best desserts in the city.
🔶 H6 ✉ Santa Teresa 10 ☎ 93 415 28 77 🕐 Closed Sat lunch and Sun 🚇 Diagonal

LAHORE (££)
This small, friendly establishment serves authentic Pakistani

cooking. The jovial Javed Iqbal Butt, who runs the place, moderates the spices of each dish according to your taste.
🔜 H5 ✉ Torrente de la Olla 159 ☎ 93 218 95 11 🄶 Closed Mon 🄼 Fontana

MADRID-BARCELONA (££)

The Catalan cuisine of this pleasingly retro establishment is always good value, particularly the lunchtime *menú del día*.
🔜 H7 ✉ Aragó 282 ☎ 93 215 70 27 🄶 Closed Sat evening, Sun and Aug 🄼 Passeig de Gràcia

MEDULIO (££)

Jose Luis Lopez serves up his fabulous brand of Galician cooking at more than reasonable prices. Complemented by an excellent wine list.
🔜 H5 ✉ Príncep d'Astúries 6 ☎ 93 217 38 68 🄶 Closed Sun evening 🄼 Fontana

L'OLIVÉ (££)

Good service and delicious Catalan meat and seafood dishes in a traditional Eixample setting.
🔜 G6 ✉ Muntaner 171 ☎ 93 430 90 27/93 322 98 47 🄶 Closed Sun evening 🄼 Hospital Clinic

OROTAVA (£££)

Although the art on the walls vies with the food for your attention, concentrate on the carefully prepared *cocina de mercado*, which could include game as well as succulent seafood. Founded in the 1930s, Orotava is one of the city's favourite eating-places.
🔜 G7 ✉ Consell de Cent 335

☎ 93 487 73 74/93 487 87 69 🄶 Closed Sun 🄼 Passeig de Gràcia

PEKÍN (££)

This is just one of the city's tasteful Chinese restaurants, with Cantonese and Beijing food to match the setting.
🔜 G6 ✉ Rossello 202 ☎ 93 215 01 77 🄶 Closed Sun evening 🄼 Diagonal

RENO (£££)

Exquisite Franco-Catalan cuisine presented with style. Reserve in advance.
🔜 G6 ✉ Tuset 27 ☎ 93 200 91 29 🄶 Closed Sat lunch 🄼 Diagonal

THAI GARDENS (££)

This has been a popular addition to the Barcelona scene, following the success of its predecessor in Madrid. The *menú degustación* is excellent.
🔜 H7 ✉ Diputació 273 ☎ 93 487 90 98 🄼 Passeig de Gràcia

LA TRAMOIA (£)

Lively brasserie on two floors at the corner of the Rambla de Catalunya and the Gran Via. It's noisy downstairs but quieter on the first floor. Window tables have a good view of life on the street below.
🔜 H7 ✉ Rambla de Catalunya 15 ☎ 93 412 36 34 🄼 Passeig de Gràcia, Catalunya

YAMADORY (£££)

The first of Barcelona's Japanese restaurants is popular with executives visiting from Asia.
🔜 G7 ✉ Aribau 68 ☎ 93 453 92 64 🄶 Closed Sun 🄼 Passeig de Gràcia

Spanish meats

Although pork is the mainstay of meat dishes, there is plenty of choice for carnivores, including brains, sweetbreads, trotters and other items that have vanished from other nations' tables. Beef and lamb are good, and game is excellent, including pheasant, partridge and wild boar (and don't ignore the humble rabbit). Try unusual combinations like duck with pears or meat with seafood.

65

BARCELONETA & PORT OLÍMPIC

Tips and taxes

There is no real fixed rate for tipping in restaurants. Some people leave a pile of whatever small coins they have in their pockets, others simply round up the bill to the nearest 100 pesetas. It is unusual to give more than a couple of hundred pesetas even in the most sophisticated places. VAT is charged at 7 per cent and is normally included in the bill.

BARCELONETA (££)
This friendly, busy restaurant delivers great value seafood, with fast and efficient service.
✚ H10 ✉ L'Escar 22 ☎ 93 221 21 11 🚇 Barceloneta

CA LA LLUISA (££)
This waterfront restaurant, with a large *terraza*, serves a wonderful *fideua* (a noodly version of the more famous paella).The *menú del día* is excellent.
✚ H10 ✉ Passeig Joan de Borbó 12 ☎ 93 225 06 95 🚇 Barceloneta

CAL PINXO (££)
The latest restaurant from the famous Pinxo family of restaurateurs offers an excellent menu. Best of the bunch of restaurants housed in the converted Palau de Mar.
✚ H9 ✉ Palau de Mar ☎ 93 221 22 11 🚇 Barceloneta

CAN COSTA (££)
One of the few relics of pre-Olympic Barcelona seafood restaurants.
✚ H10 ✉ Passeig Joan de Borbó 70 ☎ 93 221 95 11 🕐 Closed Sun evening and hols 🚇 Barceloneta

EL CANGREJO LOCO (££)
The crowds testify to the appeal of the reasonable prices on the *menú del día* of this large Port Olímpic seafood establishment.
✚ K10 ✉ Moll de Gregal (Port Olímpic) ☎ 93 221 17 48 🚇 Ciutadella

CAN MAJÓ (££)
Arguably the best of Barceloneta's seafood restaurants despite its plain decor, this is the place to sample *suquet*, the delicious Costa Brava fish and potato stew. The *arroces* (black rice) and *centellos* (crab) are also good
✚ H10 ✉ Almirall Aixada 23 ☎ 93 221 54 55/93 221 58 18 🕐 Closed Sun and evenings of hols 🚇 Barceloneta

LUNGOMARE (££)
Classic Italian fare by the foot of the Torre Mapfre at the Port Olímpic.
✚ K9 ✉ Calle de la Marina 16–18 ☎ 93 221 04 28/93 221 60 19 🕐 Closed Sun evening 🚇 Port Olímpic

EL PASSADIS D'EN PEP (£££)
There's no menu in this simplest of restaurants – just superb seafood, whatever is best and freshest today.
✚ H9 ✉ Plaça del Palau 2 ☎ 93 310 10 21 🕐 Closed Sun and hols 🚇 Barceloneta

SALAMANCA (£££)
Now in its fourth decade of serving good seafood and, more surprisingly in this part of town, Castilian hams. Open from 9AM until 1AM. A little hectic at night.
✚ H10 ✉ Almirall Cervera 34 ☎ 93 221 50 33 🚇 Barceloneta

SUQUET DE L'ALMIRALL (££)
The rice dishes are particularly good in this simply designed family-run restaurant. Large *terraza*.
✚ H10 ✉ Passeig Joan de Borbó ☎ 93 221 62 63 🕐 Closed Sun evening and Mon 🚇 Barceloneta

UPPER BARCELONA

ASADOR DE ARANDA (£££)

The distinctive roasts of Castile are served in the handsome setting of a *modernista* villa on the heights above the city. Sister branch Asador de Aranda II at Carrer Londres 94 is more centrally located in the Eixample, although not quite so grand.

✠ 113 ✉ Avinguda del Tibidabo 31 ☎ 93 417 01 33 ⊕ Closed Sun evening ⊚ Tibidabo

LA BALSA (£££)

Impeccable Catalan specialities are served here in a stylish setting just below the Tibidabo heights. The terrace offers stunning city views.

✠ G3 ✉ Infanta Isabel 4 ☎ 93 221 50 48 ⊕ Closed Sun and Mon evenings ⊚ Tibidabo

BISTROT DE SANTS (£££)

Superior Mediterranean cuisine in the Hotel Barcelo Sants, in a spruced-up part of town.

✠ A2 ✉ Plaça Països Catalans ☎ 93 490 95 95 ⊚ Sants Estacio

GAIG (£££)

Carles Gaig's eponymous restaurant, family-run since 1869, is arguably the finest in Barcelona, serving outstanding traditional Catalan dishes with a twist. The pheasant in malt whisky sauce is exquisite.

✠ L5 ✉ Pl Maragall 402 ☎ 93 429 10 17 ⊕ Mon and hols ⊚ Horta

NEICHEL (£££)

Alsatian chef Louis Neichel gives seasonal Catalan cuisine more than a touch of French *savoir-faire* here. The *menu degustación* is excellent.

✠ E4 ✉ Avinguda de Pedralbes 16 bis (Pedralbes) ☎ 93 203 84 08 ⊕ Closed Sat lunch, Sun and hols ⊚ Maria Christina

TRAM-TRAM (£££)

Another exceptional Mediterranean menu, with elegantly crafted desserts. Chef Isidre Soler is a rising star of Catalan cooking, so book ahead.

✠ F3 ✉ Major de Sarrià 121 ☎ 93 204 85 18 ⊕ Closed Sat lunch and Sun ⊚ FGC Reina Elisenda

LA VENTA (££)

One of the pleasures of eating in this spot in a quiet square on the Tibidabo is taking the *tramvía blau* and then sitting out on the *terraza* breathing in clear mountain air. A trip to the Mirablau bar next door for a *digestivo* after your meal is recommended.

✠ G1 ✉ Pl. Doctor Andreu ☎ 93 212 64 55 ⊚ FGC Avenida del Tibidabo

VIA VENETO (£££)

This innovative restaurant is attentive to every detail, and the Catalan fare is as refined as the setting is elegant. The location, in a smart part of town, attracts a clientele to match. The exclusive wine cellar and the creations of the pastry chef are outstanding.

✠ F5 ✉ Ganduxer 10–12 ☎ 93 200 70 24 ⊕ Closed Sat lunch and Sun ⊟ 63 from Plaça Universitat

Fish for all

The seafood restaurants of Barcelona, concentrated in harbourside Barceloneta, are famous. They serve *zarsuela* (a seafood stew) and *suquet de peix* (fish and potato soup) as well as *fideus* (a paella-style dish with noodles instead of rice). *Arròs negre* is rice cooked in the black ink of a squid.

Tapas Bars & Cafés

P and T

Pa amb tomàquet never fails to comfort a homesick Catalan and no meal is really complete without it. The local version of bread and butter, it consists of a slab of toasted *pa de pagès* (peasant bread) rubbed with a ripe tomato then drizzled with olive oil and spiked with a touch of garlic.

AL WAHA

Popular Gràcia venue with delicious Lebanese pitas, salads and sweets. The sister restaurant, further up the road, specialises in pizzas.
🞢 H5 ✉ Verdi 40 and 16
Ⓜ Fontana

ALT HEIDELBERG

Old Heidelberg serves substantial German dishes and beers among the more usual Spanish fare.
🞢 G8 ✉ Ronda Universitat 5
☎ 93 318 10 32
Ⓜ Universitat, Catalunya

THE BAGEL SHOP

The first place in Barcelona to sell fresh bagels and still the best. The service is laid-back in the extreme, however, so don't expect fast food.
🞢 H8 ✉ Canuda 25 ☎ 93
302 41 61 Ⓜ Catalunya

BAR CELTA

This Galician bar is one of several in Carrer de la Mercé and the side streets at the seaward end of the Barri Gòtic. It serves a huge variety of tapas. The *oreja* (pig's ear) is superb.
🞢 G/H9 ✉ Mercé 16 ☎ 93
315 00 06 Ⓒ Closed Aug
Ⓜ Drassanes

BAR DEL PI

Friendly service at this tapas bar delightfully located in the little square dominated by the church of Santa Maria del Pi.
🞢 G/H9 ✉ Place Sant Josep
Oriol Ⓜ Liceu

BAR RODRIGO

Popular Ribera tapas bar near the looming church of Santa Maria del Mar.
🞢 H9 ✉ Argenteria 67
☎ 93 310 30 20 Ⓒ Closed
Thu Ⓜ Jaume I

BODEGA SEPÚLVEDA

The excellent value *menú del día* usually includes a good seafood dish. Or make a tasty meal of the varied tapas.
🞢 G8 ✉ Sepúlveda 173bis
☎ 93 454 70 94 Ⓒ Closed
Sun Ⓜ Urgell

CAFÉ DE L'OPERA

Opera-goers and tourists fill the art-nouveau interior and terrace tables of this dignified establishment opposite the Liceu. The best bet for people-watching on the Rambla.
🞢 G9 ✉ Rambla 74 ☎ 93
317 75 85 Ⓜ Liceu

CAFÉ SALAMBÓ

This friendly café with a youngish clientele serves fine light dishes, including salads and *torrades*, toasted sandwiches with the obligatory tomato and oil. There's also a great range of brandies and whiskys. Open late.
🞢 H5 ✉ Torrijos 51 ☎ 93
218 69 66 Ⓜ Fontana

CERVECERÍA CATALANA

A great place to sample bottled beers from around the world, as well as the local brew on tap, this is one of the more popular bars in the Eixample. There are also hot and cold tapas and a good selection of salads. *Terraza* open in summer.
🞢 G7 ✉ Carrer Mallorca 236
☎ 93 216 03 68 Ⓜ Passeig
de Gràcia

FLASH-FLASH, TORTILLERÍA

Omelettes with many fillings are the focus at this popular eating place; the *menú del día* is also tempting.

➕ G6 ✉ Granada del Penedés 25 ☎ 93 237 09 90 🕐 Closed Christmas 🚇 Diagonal 🚌 16, 17, 22, 24, 28 from Plaça de Catalunya

HIVERNACLE

The elegant surroundings of the 19th-century glasshouse at the Parc de la Ciutadella are a relaxing place to stop for coffee.

➕ J9 ✉ Parc de la Ciutadella ☎ 93 268 01 77 🚇 Arc de Triomf

IRATI

Basque-style tapas (individual items, usually on bread) as well as reasonably priced lunches.

➕ G9 ✉ Cardenal Casanas 17 ☎ 93 302 30 84 🕐 Closed Sun evening and Mon 🚇 Liceu

JOSE LUIS

Barcelona is not really the heartland of the *tapa*, which may account for the huge success of the tapas temple founded by Madrid's Jose Luis. *Montaditos* (tiny sandwiches, usually of tuna and red peppers, tortilla or ham) are a must.

➕ G6 ✉ Diagonal 520 ☎ 93 200 75 63 🚇 Diagonal

PANS & COMPANY

A useful Catalan answer to fast-food, with emphasis on tomato and bread *pa amb tomàquet* (➤ 68). Various locations around the city.

➕ G8 ✉ Rambla 123 ☎ 93 301 66 21 🚇 Liceu

ELS QUATRE GATS

No visit to Barcelona is complete without a pause at this shrine of *Modernisme*. The Four Cats was frequented by Barcelona's turn-of-the-20th-century bohemian crowd (including Picasso), two of whom are depicted in the famous picture (a reproduction of arty types riding a tandem bicycle. Bar up front and a restaurant in back.

➕ H8 ✉ Montsio 3bis ☎ 93 302 41 40 🕐 Closed Sun lunch 🚇 Urquinaona, Catalunya

SCHILLING

This popular café bar, between the Rambla and the Plaça St Jaume, does great hot chocolate and sandwiches, and scoops a range of ice creams.

➕ H9 ✉ Ferran 23 ☎ 93 317 67 87 🚇 Liceu

TAPA TAPA

Central *cervecería*, with a wide selection of beers and tapas. Specials include snails, black squid, fried pig snout and octopus.

➕ H7 ✉ Passeig de Gràcia 44 ☎ 93 488 33 69 🚇 Passeig de Gràcia

EL XAMPANYET

Along with the house speciality *xamparya* (a sweetish, sparkling wine), draft beer and wine flow freely in this lively champagne bar on medieval Carrer de Montcada near the Picasso Museum. Good tapas.

➕ H9 ✉ Montcada 22 ☎ 93 319 70 03 🕐 Closed Mon 🚇 Jaume 1

Different drinks

Barcelona tapwater is drinkable, but not particularly appetising. Most people are prepared to pay that little extra for mineral water *amb gas* (with bubbles) or *sense gas* (still). A soft drink unique to Spain is *horchata* (*orxata* in Catalan), a milk-like drink extruded from the crushed nut called a *chufa*. It takes a little getting used to but is deliciously refreshing once you have acquired the taste.

69

MALLS & DEPARTMENT STORES

More than a mall

Spain seems to have caught on to Anglo-Saxon ideas of supermarkets and shopping malls relatively late. First to arrive in Barcelona were the elegant Eixample malls specialising in fashion. Now there are monster malls like Glòries, plugged in to the suburban expressway network. Interesting enough in themselves, they hardly compete with the experience of shopping on the waterfront in the Old Port's Maremagnum.

EL CORTE INGLÉS

Synonymous in Spain with the concept of the department store, the Corte Inglés has no competition in Barcelona; virtually everything you could ever need is here under the roof of an aircraft-carrier-like establishment on Plaça de Catalunya. On the several floors between the splendid supermarket in the basement and the eagle's-nest eating place at the top are designer fashions, perfumes, cosmetics, jewellery, a hairdressers, handicrafts, a stationers, a bookshop, a travel bureau and an interpreter service.
🕂 H8 ✉ Plaça de Catalunya 14
☎ 93 306 38 00 🚇 Catalunya

MALLS

BULEVARD ROSA

The prototype of Barcelona's fashion malls, the Bulevard Rosa boasts 100-plus boutiques with the best in fashion, shoes and accessories.
🕂 H7 ✉ Passeig de Gràcia 53–5 (also at Diagonal 474)
☎ 93 309 06 50 🚇 Passeig de Gràcia

LES GLÒRIES

More than 200 shops at the eastern end of the Diagonal, including international names, and an excellent supermarket, the Continente.
🕂 K7 ✉ Diagonal 280
☎ 93 486 04 04 🚇 Glòries

MAREMAGNUM

Best approached via the Rambla del Mar and the southwest entrance with a spectacular mirror canopy, Maremagnum, in the middle of the Old Port, contains not only fashion boutiques, but also gift stores, cafés, restaurants, bars and nightspots.
🕂 G10/11 ✉ Moll d'Espanya
☎ 93 225 81 00 🚇 Drassanes

EL TRIANGLE

New complex on the Plaça Catalunya, containing – amongst other stores – FNAC and Habitat. FNAC is one of the city's best sources for books, with a large English section, videos and compact discs. The huge perfume and cosmetics shop, Sephora, takes up the whole basement floor and is invariably crowded, and there is also a branch of the popular men's fashion chain Massimo Dutti. The complex has an inexpensive café with a *terraza*.
🕂 H8 ✉ Plaça Catalunya 4
☎ 93 344 18 00 🚇 Catalunya

DRUGSTORES

DEPASO

One of a chain of stores that stay open until the small hours offering everything you might have overlooked during the day: food, music, magazines, newspapers.
🕂 G7 ✉ Muntaner 14 ☎ 93 454 58 46 🚇 Universitat

VIP'S

Another late-night opener with a whole range of goods including books. There is a restaurant, too.
🕂 H8 ✉ Rambla de Catalunya 7–9 ☎ 93 317 49 23
🚇 Catalunya

ARTS, CRAFTS & DESIGN

ART ESCUDELLERS

Colourful ceramics from all over Spain as well as cured Iberian hams. You can also do some wine-tasting in the store's bodega.

📍 G9 ✉ Escudellers 23 ☎ 93 412 68 01 🚇 Liceu

4ART MONTFALCON

Picture-framing is a speciality of this attractive shop along with handmade jewellery and decorated plates and T-shirts.

📍 H8 ✉ Boters 4 ☎ 93 301 13 25 🚇 Liceu

ASPECTOS

The real thing in a Barcelona household funishings design store, with the work of some already established designers, as well as the young and up-and-coming.

📍 H9 ✉ Rec 28 ☎ 93 319 52 85 🚇 Jaume I

B D EDICIONES DE DISEÑO

A virtual museum of modern furniture design from the likes of Charles Rennie Mackintosh and Antoní Gaudí to the more contemporary Ricardo Bofill, in a building by Domènech i Montaner.

📍 H7 ✉ Mallorca 291 ☎ 93 458 69 09 🚇 Passeig de Gràcia

DOS I UNA

An early proponent of contemporary design, this establishment is filled with superior gift items.

📍 H6 ✉ Rosselló 275 ☎ 93 217 70 32 🚇 Diagonal

GOTHAM

Restored furniture and an eclectic selection of lamps from the 1950s, 60s and 70s, as well as many art-deco pieces.

📍 09 ✉ Cervantes 7 ☎ 93 412 46 47 🚇 Jaume I

INSOLIT

One of a kind objects of great originality.

📍 H6 ✉ Diagonal 353 ☎ 93 207 49 19 🚇 Verdaguer

LA MANUAL ALPARGATERA

All kinds of woven items, some created before your eyes. The speciality: handmade espadrilles.

📍 H9 ✉ Avinyó 7 ☎ 93 301 01 72 🚇 Liceu

MOSTRA PERMANENT D'ARTESANÍA

An official outlet for local Catalan crafts, with ever-changing displays of varied handmade objects.

📍 G7 ✉ Passeig de Gràcia ☎ 93 215 71 78 🚇 Passeig de Gràcia

NEOCERAMICA

Spanish and international ceramic floor and wall tiles.

📍 G3 ✉ Mandri 43 ☎ 93 211 89 58 🚇 La Bonanova 🚌 14 from Plaça de Catalunya

PILMA

Another good outlet for decorative and designer objects for the home.

📍 H6 ✉ Diagonal 403 ☎ 93 416 13 99 🚇 Diagonal

VINÇON

Every kind of domestic design, from furniture to fabrics to bathroom and kitchen fittings. A Barcelona institution since the 1960s.

📍 H6 ✉ Passeig de Gràcia 96 ☎ 93 215 60 50 🚇 Diagonal

What to buy in the Barri Gòtic

The intricate streets and alleyways of the old town east of the Rambla are full of individual shops selling virtually everything you might want to either eat or admire. There are craftsman's candles, cured hams and all kinds of antiques and art objects. Portaferrissa and Portal de l'Angel streets have fashion and shoe shops.

FASHION

Elegant shopping in the Eixample

For many visitors, Barcelona's main attraction is its stylish fashion shops. The most prestigious shopping area is in the Eixample, in the area between Gran Via de les Corts Catalanes, Carrer de Balmes, Passeig de Gràcia and Avinguda Diagonal. If you can't afford what's on offer, window shopping is an experience to be savoured, not only for the quality and sophisticated display of the goods but also for the many *modernista* buildings in the area.

ADOLFO DOMÍNGUEZ
Spain's brightest fashion star, renowned for linen suits, designed the store as well as the super-stylish (and pricey) clothes.
✚ H7 ✉ Passeig de Gràcia 89 (and at three other locations in the city centre) ☎ 93 215 13 39 🚇 Passeig de Gràcia

ANTONIO MIRÓ
One of Spain's top designers, Miró is best known for his men's fashions, but he also has a range of women's and children's clothes, shoes, eyeglasses and furniture.
✚ H7 ✉ Carrer Consell de Cent 349–351 ☎ 93 487 06 70 🚇 Passeig de Gràcia

CACHE CACHE
Natty togs for toddlers and older children.
✚ H7 ✉ Valencia 282 ☎ 93 215 40 07 🚇 Passeig de Gràcia

CATIMINI
Attractive children's clothes shop. Displays are all colour-coordinated to help you match outfits.
✚ H6 ✉ Passeig de Gracia 100 ☎ 93 215 77 94 🚇 Diagonal

CONTRIBUCIONES Y MODA
Step into high fashion (albeit last year's models, but who'll notice?) at a bargain price.
✚ H6 ✉ Riera de Sant Miquel 30 ☎ 93 218 71 40 🚇 Diagonal

D409
Classic, elegant designs for women in an equally chic setting on the Diagonal, just off the Rambla Catalunya.
✚ H6 ✉ Diagonal 409 ☎ 93 415 44 33 🚇 Diagonal

DAVID VALLS
Original knitwear with eye-catching colours, styles and textures.
✚ H7 ✉ Valencia 235 ☎ 93 487 12 85 🚇 Passeig de Gràcia

ESCADA
Women's high fashion direct from Italy, with prices to match. Similarly elegant designs available in sister store Laurels next door.
✚ H7 ✉ Passeig de Gràcia 77–79 ☎ 93 467 41 70 🚇 Passeig de Gràcia

GABRIEL TORRES
Men's designer clothes reflecting a contemporary Japanese influence.
✚ H6 ✉ Lluis Antunez 8 ☎ 93 217 16 61 🚇 Diagonal

GONZALO COMELLA
After dressing three generations of Barcelona's affluent, this institution is changing with the times and you'll find far more designer labels.
✚ H7 ✉ Passeig de Gràcia 6 ☎ 93 412 66 00 🚇 Passeig de Gràcia

GROC
Tempting creations for both men and women by Catalonia's favourite designer, Toni Mirò.
✚ H6 ✉ Rambla de Catalunya 100bis (also – women's wear only – at Muntaner 385) ☎ 93 215 01 80 🚇 Diagonal

ÍNTIMO DUE
Luxurious lingerie and exclusive underwear.

✚ H7 ✉ Pau Claris 113
☎ 93 487/ 69 25 Ⓜ Passeig
de Gràcia

JEAN-PIERRE BUA

Barcelona's most chic
(and wealthy) queue up
here each season for
creations as startling as
the stylish decor.
✚ G5 ✉ Diagonal 469
☎ 93 439 71 00 Ⓜ Urgell

LÍDIA DELGADO

A collection of stylish
clothes for women from
local Barcelona designer
Lídia Delgado.
✚ H6 ✉ Carrer Minerva 21
☎ 93 415 99 98 Ⓜ Gràcia

MANGO

Nationwide chain of
women's fashion stores
with attractive, well-made
clothes in good fabrics at
affordable prices. There
are several branches
throughout the city.
✚ H7 ✉ Passeig de Gràcia 65
☎ 93 215 75 30 Ⓜ Passeig
de Gràcia

MASSIMO DUTTI

Natty designs at more
than reasonable prices in
this nationwide outlet.
Shirts are a speciality.
✚ G6 ✉ Via Augusta 33
☎ 93 217 73 06 Ⓜ Diagonal

MILANO

Stylish men's suits, jackets
and overcoats at bargain
prices. Very popular.
✚ G8 ✉ La Rambla 138
☎ 93 317 47 12 Ⓜ Drassanes

MOSSELLA

Classic men's fashions –
lots of tweed and striped
shirts with plain collars.
The store has been open in
the basement of Gaudí's

La Pedrera since 1920.
✚ H6 ✉ Passeig de Gràcia 92
☎ 93 215 33 52 Ⓜ Diagonal

SANTACANA

Slinky silk and satin
underwear for men and
women, as well as elegant
swimwear.
✚ G7 ✉ Rambla de Catalunya
90 ☎ 93 215 04 21
Ⓜ Diagonal/Passeig de Gràcia

STOCKLAND

End-of-line designer
fashions at attractive prices.
✚ H8 ✉ Comtal 22 ☎ 93
318 03 31 Ⓜ Urquinaona

VEHILS

Smart but casual fashion
for men and women, with
a tailoring service upstairs.
A sportswear section is in
the basement.
✚ H8 ✉ Avenguda del Portal
de l'Angel 32–34 ☎ 93 317 80
82 Ⓜ Catalunya

ZARA

This mass operation is
now a national and
international success story,
with shops all over
Europe. The designs are
up-to-the-minute and well
priced. The attractive
three-storey shop near
Place Catalunya should
be your first stop if you
want a bargain, but there
are branches city-wide.
✚ G8 ✉ Pelai 58 ☎ 93 301
09 68 Ⓜ Catalunya

ZSU-ZSA

Tiny shop selling original
clothes from some of
Barcelona's trendiest
young designers, often at
greatly reduced prices.
Good place for a bargain.
✚ H9 ✉ Avinyo 50 ☎ 93
412 49 65 Ⓜ Jaume I

Desirables of the Diagonal

A zone of fine shops extends
along the great avenue known as
the Diagonal between Plaça Joan
Carles I and Plaça Francesc Macià.
Just off the avenue is one of the
city's most fashionable shopping
streets, Avinguda Pau Casals; in
these shops and adjacent
shopping malls, those who would
like to consider themselves a cut
above the common herd on
downtown Rambla, can be seen.

SHOES & ACCESSORIES

Fine design

Barcelona's design tradition and its endless array of unusual and individual shops make the hunt for gifts and accessories unusally enjoyable. Fine leather goods at reasonable prices are to be found everywhere in the Eixample, and there are numerous expensive jewellery shops. In the Old Town, look for hand-painted jewellery, porcelain and wooden crafts.

BALLY
Fine footwear and all manner of other leather goods for both sexes.
✚ H7 ✉ Passeig de Gràcia 30 ☎ 93 412 70 08 🚇 Passeig de Gràcia

CAMPER
Male and female, everyone in Barcelona seems to have a pair of Camper's well-made, comfortable and stylish shoes. You can buy them in a handful of shops around the city and in department stores, including El Corte Ingles.
✚ H7 ✉ Valencia 249 (also at Pau Casals 5 and Muntaner 248) ☎ 93 215 63 90 🚇 Passeig de Gràcia

HIPÒTESIS
Outstanding modern jewellery by Spanish and international designers.
✚ H6 ✉ Rambla de Catalunya 105 ☎ 93 215 02 98 🚇 Provença

JOAQUIN BERAO
Original jewellery by a wonderful Spanish designer.
✚ H6 ✉ Rosselló 277 ☎ 93 218 61 87 🚇 Diagonal

LOEWE
World-renowned specialists in skins, Loewe's is known for its leather clothes, handbags, wallets and suitcases. The store occupies one of the finest buildings on Passeig de Gràcia: Domènech i Montaner's Casa Lleo Morera.
✚ H7 ✉ Passeig de Gràcia 35 (also at Diagonal 570, Plaça Pio XII, and Juan Sebastian Bach 8) ☎ 93 216 04 00 🚇 Passeig de Gràcia

OPTICA 2000
In addition to spectacles and contact lenses, this store carries all the top names in sunglasses, including Gucci, Dolce & Gabbana and Calvin Klein.
✚ H7 ✉ Consell de Cent 310 ☎ 93 288 02 26 🚇 Passeig de Gràcia

PUIG DORIA
Exclusive designs in watches, rings, bracelets and other jewellery.
✚ H7 ✉ Rambla de Catalunya 88 (also at Diagonal 612) ☎ 93 215 10 90 🚇 Passeig de Gràcia

ROYALTY
Huge selection of footwear by all the top names as well as the store's own designers. There's a new collection each season.
✚ H8 ✉ Avenguida del Portal de l'Angel 38 ☎ 93 317 16 32 🚇 Metro Catalunya

SOLÉ
This store on an appropriately named street specialises in footware in larger sizes.
✚ G9 ✉ Ample 7 ☎ 93 301 69 84 🚇 Drassanes

SUPERGA
Shoes in great designs and unexpectedly bright colours for children and adults, as well as rucksacks, shorts and jackets.
✚ H6 ✉ Rambla de Catalunya 90 ☎ 93 215 37 12 🚇 Diagonal

YANKO
Classy, expensive and beautifully designed shoes.
✚ H7 ✉ Passeig de Gràcia 95 ☎ 93 487 96 96 🚇 Passeig de Gràcia

BOOKS & MUSIC

ALTAÏR
A profusion of books and maps on destinations worldwide, including Barcelona, Catalonia and Spain.
✚ G7 ✉ Balmes 69–71 ☎ 93 454 29 66 🚇 Provença

BCN BOOKS
Good selection of classics and modern fiction from around the world in English, as well as teaching materials and foreign language dictionaries. Well worth a browse when you've run out of reading material.
✚ H6 ✉ Provença 291 ☎ 93 476 33 43 🚇 Diagonal

CASTELLÓ
A chain of music shops with varying specialities: the branch in Nou de la Rambla concentrates on pop, folk and world music; the branch at Tallers 3 specialises in classical music.
✚ G9 ✉ Nou de la Rambla 15 (and at Tallers 3) ☎ 93 302 42 36 🚇 Liceu

COME IN
The city's biggest selection of books in English on all subjects.
✚ G6 ✉ Provença 203 ☎ 93 453 12 04 🚇 Provença

CRISOL
Books (including titles in English), foreign-language papers and periodicals, discs and videos on two floors. Open late.
✚ G7 ✉ Rambla de Catalunya 81 (and at Consell de Cent 341) ☎ 93 215 27 20 🚇 Passeig de Gràcia

HAPPY BOOKS
A literary supermarket with books piled high – look out for some at bargain prices.
✚ G8 ✉ Pelai 20 (and at Passeig de Gràcia 77 and Provença 286) ☎ 93 317 07 68 🚇 Catalunya

LAIE
The ultimate literary café, with a wonderful selection of books downstairs, including travel maps and guides. Atmospheric bar and eatery upstairs complete with periodicals to peruse.
✚ H//8 ✉ Pau Claris 85 ☎ 93 302 73 10 🚇 Passeig de Gràcia

LIBRERIA FRANCESA
A broad, fascinating array of books in many languages. Good selection of travel books.
✚ G7 ✉ Passeig de Gràcia 91 ☎ 93 215 14 17 🚇 Passeig de Gràcia

LIBRERIA HERDER
A superbly serious bookshop with impeccable academic credentials. Strengths are in languages and science and there are many international publications (particularly in German).
✚ G7 ✉ Balmes 26 ☎ 93 317 05 78 🚇 Passeig de Gràcia, Universitat

PLANET MUSIC
Barcelona's best all-round music store has three branches, the biggest on a single floor at Mallorca 214. The jazz section, in particular, stands out.
✚ G7 ✉ Mallorca 214 ☎ 93 451 42 88 🚇 Diagonal

Reading habits
There are plenty of bookshops in Barcelona and many of them stock publications in foreign languages (especially English). Newsstands are crammed with magazines dealing with every conceivable subject, including the adult comics which seem to fascinate Spanish readers. Always prominent is the phenomenally successful glossy *Hola!*, whose preoccupation with the doings of the rich and famous has spawned imitators like the British *Hello!*

FOOD SHOPS & MARKETS

Picnic places

Look out for the offerings from the *forn de pa* (bakery) and the *xarcutería* (charcuterie or delicatessen). Don't miss slicings from a good *jamón serrano* (dry-cured ham). Look for *fuet* (a hard Catalan sausage), *chorizo*, *sobrasada* (a Mallorcan paste of pork and paprika) and cured *Manchego* cheese.

LA BOQUERIA

A city landmark, this superb market hall was built in the 19th century to house the food stalls that cluttered up the Rambla and its surrounding streets. Beyond the market's gaping entrance arch are countless stalls piled high with every foodstuff from the Mediterranean and its Catalonian hinterland. Amidst the riot of colour and smells, marvel at a hundred species of fish, gorgeous vegetables, fragrant herbs, and animal parts that you may not have dreamed existed – all temptingly arranged.
G8 ⊠ Rambla 91 ☎ 93 318 25 84 🚇 Liceu

CASA GISPERT

Founded in the 1850s, this establishment is an expert roaster of nuts and coffees, and purveys everything from fresh-roasted hazelnuts and almonds to Iranian pistachios.
H9 ⊠ Sombrerers 319 ☎ 93 319 75 35 🚇 Jaume I

COLMADO QUILEZ

An emporium of fine tinned and bottled foodstuffs from Spain and Europe, together with an array of cheeses, hams and other delicacies, and a variety of alcoholic drinks.
H9 ⊠ Rambla de Catalunya 63 ☎ 93 215 23 56 🚇 Passeig de Gràcia

ESCRIBA PASTISSERIES

The city's most delicious creations in chocolate lie behind the *modernista* shopfront of the Antigua Casa Figueras.
G8 ⊠ Rambla 83 (also at Gran Via de les Corts Catalanes 546) ☎ 93 301 60 27 🚇 Liceu

FORMATGERÍA CIRERA

Relatively little known abroad, Spanish cheeses are well worth trying, particularly those available from such specialists as this one.
G8 ⊠ Cera 45 ☎ 93 441 07 59 🚇 Sant Antoni

FORN DE PA SANT JORDI

One of the city's many *forns* (ovens) turns out mouth-watering home-made breads, pastries and cakes.
H9 ⊠ Llibreteria 8 ☎ 93 310 40 16 🚇 Jaume I

MERCAT DE L'ABACERIA CENTRAL

Although lacking the enormous range of products available at the Boqueria, there are plenty of stalls selling all manner of fresh produce in this market – and it's less touristy.
F5 ⊠ Mallorca ☎ 93 247 00 42 🚍 41 from Plaça de Catalunya

VINS I CAVES LA CATEDRAL

One of the most convenient places to increase your understanding and appreciation of the wines of Catalonia and the rest of Spain.
H8 ⊠ Plaça de Ramon Berenguer el Gran 1 ☎ 93 319 07 27 🚇 Jaume I

GIFTS & ANTIQUES

BARRI GÒTIC ANTIQUES MARKET
Bric-à-brac rather than heirloom bargains dominate the stalls in front of the cathedral.
➕ H8 ✉ Avinguda de la Catedral 6 ☎ 93 291 61 18 🕐 Thu 9–8 🚇 Jaume I

BIOSCA I BOTEY
Stunning array of lighting, from bedside lamps to chandeliers, including a range of original designs.
➕ H6 ✉ Rambla de Catalunya 129 ☎ 93 415 34 44 🚇 Diagonal

BULEVARD DELS ANTIQUARIS
Every kind of antique dealer can be found in this complex of over 70 shops next to the Bulevard Rosa mall.
➕ H7 ✉ Passeig de Gràcia 55 ☎ 93 215 44 99 🚇 Passeig de Gràcia

CASA CONSISTORIAL/ ARTESANÍA MARCO
The Spanish Village, where this is located (➤ 29), may itself seem like a huge gift shop but the huge array of handmade ship models here is varied and very reasonably priced.
➕ E8 ✉ Pueblo Espanyol, Mercaders 4–6 ☎ 93 423 93 95 🚇 Espanya 🚌 13, 61

CERÁMICA VILLEGAS
The most comprehensive choice of pots of all kinds, from rustic to refined.
➕ H8 ✉ Comtal 31 ☎ 93 317 53 30 🚇 Urquinaona

ELS ENCANTS FLEA MARKET
Patient searching can reveal gold among the dross of worn clothing, broken furniture and other unwanted items. Plan your visit for around 8AM for the best selection.
➕ K7 ✉ Plaça de les Glòries ☎ 93 246 30 30 🕐 Mon, Wed, Fri and Sat 8–7 🚇 Glòries

ITEMS D'HO
Original gadgets and gizmos of all kinds.
➕ H7 ✉ Passeig de Gràcia 55 (Bulevard Rosa) ☎ 93 216 09 41 🚇 Passeig de Gràcia

PLAÇA REIAL: COIN AND STAMP MARKET
The Plaça Reial plays host every Sunday to stallholders and collector types indulging their enthusiasms.
➕ G9 ✉ Plaça Reial ☎ 93 291 61 18 🕐 Sun 9–2:30 🚇 Liceu

PLAÇA DE SANT JOSEP ORIOL: PICTURE MARKET
Barcelona's appealing counterpart to Paris's Montmartre art market takes place in one of the Barri Gòtic's most picturesque squares on Sundays. Worth a browse.
➕ G9 ✉ Plaça de Sant Josep Oriol ☎ 93 291 61 00 🕐 Sun 9–2 🚇 Liceu

POPULART
Gift shop opened in the 1960s by a group of artists keen to revive traditional art methods. Ingenious objects made from all kinds of materials complement the cards and posters. Just down the road from the Picasso Museum.
➕ H9 ✉ Montcada 22 ☎ 93 310 78 49 🚇 Jaume I

Golden gifts
Among the touristy shops of the Spanish Village – the Poble Espanyol (➤ 29) – keep an eye peeled for gold: you can watch metalworkers and others actually producing some of the items for sale and there are outlets for unusual and original gifts and souvenirs.

Bars, Discos & Clubs

Night zones

Vigorous nightlife takes place all over the city. Plaça Reial in the old town is always active, and the waterfront has really come alive with the opening of the Maremagnum shopping, restaurant and entertainment complex and the development of the Port Olímpic, where the action continues to dawn and beyond. There is a concentration of designer bars in the Eixample and Gràcia, with some of the smoother venues on the exclusive slopes of the wealthy suburb of Tibidabo.

BIKINI
This large club in the basement of the L'Illa shopping mall has separate spaces for cocktails, salsa and rock.
✚ F5 ✉ Déu I Mata 105 ☎ 93 322 00 05 Ⓜ Les Corts

LA BOÎTE
An eclectic mix of soul, funk, hip-hop and Motown classics are on the turntable. Occasional live music.
✚ G6 ✉ Diagonal 477 ☎ 93 419 59 50 Ⓜ Diagonal

GIMLET
The granddaddy of 1950s-style American bars serves cool cocktails in an impeccably sober setting.
✚ G5 ✉ Santaló 46 ☎ 93 201 53 06 Ⓜ Hospital Clínic

I QUÈ?
This up-and-coming bar is just off the Plaça Diamant in Gràcia. A youngish crowd has made it a popular meeting place before trips downtown on weekends – it's more sedate mid-week.
✚ H5 ✉ Topazi 6 ☎ 93 416 07 33 Ⓜ Fontana

KARMA
This basement venue is still the most popular of several lively rock clubs around Plaça Reial.
✚ G9 ✉ Plaça Reial 10 ☎ 93 302 56 80 Ⓜ Liceu

KGB
This stark shed of a building styled on a secret police theme attracts the hardiest of clubbing night-owls; the action really begins only when dawn is approaching.
✚ J5 ✉ Alegre de Dalt 55 ☎ 93 210 59 06 Ⓜ Joanic/Alfons X

LONDON BAR
Here since 1910, this former bohemian favourite, later taken up by local hippies, now draws an interesting, cosmopolitan mix of locals and young foreign residents. There's a stage at one end of the cavernous gallery, and occasional live music.
✚ G9 ✉ Nou de la Rambla 34 ☎ 93 318 52 61 Ⓜ Paral.lel

MOOG
Techno goes full blast at one of the city's trendiest clubs. Look for guest DJs from the international circuit. Chill-out room.
✚ G9 ✉ Arc del Teatre 3 ☎ 93 318 59 66 Ⓜ Drassanes

NETWORK
Designers Eduardo Samso and Alfredo Arribas made Network a compulsory stop on the bar circuit with their high-tech interior inspired by futuristic films like *Blade Runner*.
✚ F5 ✉ Diagonal 616 ☎ 93 414 05 32 🚌 41 from Plaça de Catalunya

NICK HAVANNA
A classic among Barcelona's designer bars. Nick Havanna's successful formula has been reproduced many times since the mid-1980s. The place may have lost some of its edge but its still well worth a stop for a drink.
✚ G6 ✉ Rosselló 208 ☎ 93 215 65 91 Ⓜ Diagonal/Provença

ON/OFF

Spaced-out survivors of the weekend's revels flee the light of day in this large club behind the Poble Espanyol, where the action only really begins after 4AM.

🔆 E8 ✉ Comide de la Fuxarda ☎ 93 450 33 20 🚇 Espanya, then 🚌 13,61

OTTO ZUTZ

This improbably named club in a three-storey warehouse is still the place to see and be seen for Barcelona's glitterati and those aspiring to join them. Clever lighting and metal staircases and galleries set the scene. Zutz was a German dentist who pulled teeth just up the road.

🔆 H5 ✉ Lincoln 15 ☎ 93 238 07 22 🚇 Gràcia

PARTYCULAR

The gardens of this big villa on the slopes below Tibidabo make it a favourite summer venue, though it is a fair climb up along the Tramvia Blau route from Tibidabo station. Great views across the funfair and the city.

🔆 H2 ✉ Tibidabo 61 ☎ 93 211 62 61 🚇 Tibidabo

TORRES DE AVILA

Design wizards Alfred Arribas and Javier Mariscal conjured up this magical series of symbol-loaded spaces in the twin towers guarding the entrance to the Poble Espanyol. Trance-techno discos are staged here at weekends. In summer, when dancing palls, there is a stunning view over the city from the rooftop terrace, with refreshing sea breezes.

🔆 D8 ✉ Marquès de Comillas (Poble Espanyol) ☎ 93 424 93 09 🚇 Espanya 🚌 13, 61

SNOOKER

Stylish cocktail bar with a trendy clientele, an eclectic mix of music and snooker tables. Open until late.

🔆 H8 ✉ Roger de Llúria 42 ☎ 93 317 97 60 🚇 Urquinaona

UP AND DOWN

Still frequented by those from the upper end of the social scale, this club caters to an older set upstairs, where the action is mainly admiring younger revelers' antics down on the lower dance floor.

🔆 E5 ✉ Numancia 179 ☎ 93 205 51 94 🚇 Maria Christina

VELVET

Designer Arribas indulged himself in an extravagant variety of materials and textures in creating a retro atmosphere in this larger than average disco bar.

🔆 G6 ✉ Balmes 161 ☎ 93 217 67 14 🚇 Provença/Diagonal

ZSA ZSA

A *tour-de-force* of design with spectacular lighting effects and equally spectacular cocktails, much appreciated by an older-than-average crowd. Fresh fruit shakes are a house speciality.

🔆 G6 ✉ Rosselló 156 ☎ 93 453 85 66 🚇 Provença

Designer metropolis

Evidence of Barcelona's position at the sharp end of contemporary design can be seen all over the city, in squares, parks, street furniture, shop-fronts and interiors — even in the way gifts are packaged. In the 1980s, these talents were turned to the design of nightspots, each of which sought to upstage the rest

FILM, THEATRE & MUSIC

Pau Casals

The great Catalan cellist, better known to the world as Pablo Casals (1876–1973), was a Catalan. In 1920 he helped push Barcelona onto Europe's musical map by founding his Barcelona Orchestra, which performed regularly in the Palau de la Música. In 1924–25 Igor Stravinsky directed the orchestra in concerts featuring his own works.

CINEMAS

Film-going is very popular in Spain, and lines are constant outside theatres before shows begin. Most first-run films are dubbed into Spanish or Catalan, but somewhere in town you can probably find a showing in the original version, especially in Gràcia's Verdi and Verdi Park cinemas and in the Icària Yelmo complex at the Port Olímpic. Look in the listings for the notation VO (*versión original*).

FILMOTECA DE LA GENERALITAT DE CATALUNYA

The well-intentioned equivalent of a national film theatre, with themed programmes of new and classic films, invariably in the original version.

⊞ F5 ✉ Cinema Aquitania, Avinguda de Sarrià 31–33 ☎ 93 410 75 90 🕒 Closed hols and Aug 🚇 Hospital Clínic

COMPANIES AND ENSEMBLES

AUDITORI

This impressive new venue provides a home for l'Orquestra, Simfònica de Barcelona i National de Catalunya.

⊞ K8 ✉ Lepant 150 ☎ 93 317 10 96 🚇 Glòries

ELS COMEDIANTS

When not entertaining audiences abroad, the Comedians amaze fellow *Barcelonins* with an astonishing array of music, mime, dance and tricks, often in the open air.

CENTRE CULTURAL DE LA CAIXA

The savings bank and Barcelona institution known as La Caixa has a vigorous cultural programme that includes chamber concerts in one of its prestigious properties, the Casa Macaya, a *modernista* masterpiece by architect Puig I Cadafalch.

⊞ J7 ✉ Passeig de Sant Joan 108 ☎ 93 458 89 07 🚇 Verdaguer

LA CUBANA

The original and best of the many groups mixing theatre, music, dance and mime, La Cubana was founded in 1980 by Jordi Milan as a street theatre group. The original show, which ran for four years and was seen by over a million people, propelled the group to the heady heights of their own television show. They tour and perform at various venues and are now preparing a new act, incorporating cinema and improvisation.

ELS FURA DEL BAUS

The highly talented Vermin of the Sewer perform at several venues around the city, with shows intended to maintain the shock of their name.

GRAN TEATRE DEL LICEU

Destroyed by fire in 1861, swiftly rebuilt, then burned again in 1994, the Lyceum holds a special place in the hearts of musical *Barcelonins*, since it was here that the city's passion for opera found its prime expression. The rebuilt Liceu occupies an entire block on the Lower Rambla and the opera is back full force.

 G9 ✉ Rambla 61–65 ☎ 93 485 99 00 Ⓜ Liceu

ELS JOGLARS

The Minstrels turn the Catalan talent in dance and mime to good account in often startling satires.

MERCAT DE LES FLORS

The splendid halls of the old flower market at the foot of Montjuïc now serve as the main venue for the annual Grec Festival (➤ 22). During the rest of the year there is a rich variety of dramatic, dance and concert events.

✚ E8 ✉ Lleida 59 ☎ 93 318 85 99 Ⓜ Espanya

ORFEÓ

A primary focus of the Catalan revival around the 1900s (the Palau de la Música was built for them), the Orfeó choir still plays an important role in the city's cultural life, with its repertoire of great classical works.

ORQUESTRA SIMFÒNICA DE BARCELONA I NACIONAL DE CATALUNYA

Now often known simply as 'L'Orquestra', this orchestra is an object of pride in Barcelona and Catalonia as a whole, and receives financial support from both city and region. In addition to playing standard classical

repertoire, the orchestra is also committed to showcasing little-known Catalan contributions to serious music.

PALAU DE LA MÚSICA CATALANA (➤ 38)

One of the city's unmissable architectural sights, Domènech i Montaner's Palace of Music has long been Barcelona's principal auditorium, a splendid setting for performances by the Orfeó choir, the Orquestra Simfònica and others. Book early.

✚ H8 ✉ Sant Francesc de Paula 2 ☎ 93 268 10 00 Ⓜ Urquinaona

THEATRE LLIURE

The Free Theatre, housed in a fine old Gràcia building, is the home of the well-established but progressive company of the same name, which has built its reputation on productions – in Catalan – of classical and contemporary drama. The theatre also hosts dance and poetry events and concerts of 20th-century music, and has a friendly café-restaurant.

✚ H5 ✉ Montseny 47 ☎ 93 218 92 51 Ⓜ Fontana

TEATRE NACIONAL DE CATALUNYA

Built in the undistinguished Plaça de les Glòries Catalanes, Ricardo Bofill's massive new temple of theatre is a post-modern homage to classical Greek prototypes.

✚ K8 ✉ Plaça de les arts 1 ☎ 93 306 57 00 Ⓖ Guided tours on request Ⓜ Glòries

Barcelona–Bayreuth

A century ago a surge of Wagner mania swept Barcelona and his operas remain popular today. The composer's romanticism and his ability to evoke a mythical German past struck a chord with Catalans engaged in reviving their neglected and suppressed nationhood; it was all too easy to identify the dragon as the common foe of Siegfried and St George, Catalonia's patron saint.

POPULAR MUSIC

Jazz roots

Barcelona's love affair with jazz goes back to the days before the Civil War, when Jack Hylton's dance band played at the International Exhibition and Django Reinhardt and Stéphane Grappelli brought the music of the Hot Club de France to the Hot Club de Barcelone. The tradition has been kept alive by such figures as the brilliant pianist Tete Monoliú and newcomer saxophonist Billy McHenry, and by the city's October Jazz Festival.

ANTILLA COSMOPOLITA

Lively and live Latin-American fare. The city's most popular venue of this type.
✚ G6 ⊠ Muntaner 244
☎ 93 200 77 14 ◻ 58,64

BLUES CAFÉ

Live blues a couple of times a week, performed by local acts in an intimate Gràcia setting. Serves draught Guinness and Budvar.
✚ H5 ⊠ La Perla 37 ☎ 93 416 09 65 Ⓜ Fontana

CLUB APOLO

Salsa and similar sounds fill this club in a former music hall.
✚ F/G9 ⊠ Nou de la Rambla 113 ☎ 93 441 40 01 Ⓜ Paral.lel

LA COVA DEL DRAC

Barcelona's most venerable jazz establishment has a reputation for first-rate live music.
✚ G4 ⊠ Vallmajor 33 ☎ 93 200 70 32 Ⓜ Muntaner

ESTADI OLÍMPIC

The huge capacity of the Olympic Stadium makes it the appropriate venue for visiting mega-stars such as U2 and the Rolling Stones. Tickets are best obtained through record stores.
✚ E9 ⊠ Avinguda de l'Estadi ☎ 93 425 49 49 Ⓜ Espanya, then ◻ 61

HARLEM JAZZ CLUB

Intimate and popular Barri Gòtic club that's big with local and international jazz musicians.
✚ H9 ⊠ Comtessa de Sobradiel 8 ☎ 93 310 07 55 Ⓜ Jaume I

JAMBOREE

An underground jazz club that's almost cave-like, hosting blues, soul, jazz, funk and occasional hip-hop live bands. At 1AM on weekends, the dance floor opens and gets very crowded quite quickly. Upstairs is Los Tarantos, a bar with predominantly Spanish music.
✚ G9 ⊠ Plaça Reial 17 ☎ 93 301 75 64 Ⓜ Liceu

JAZZ SI CLUB/CAFÉ

A small café with an even smaller stage high in the Raval near the San Antonio market. Affiliated with Barcelona's contemporary music school, it offers live and recorded music.
✚ G9 ⊠ Requesens 2 ☎ 93 329 00 20 Ⓜ Sant Antoni

LUZ DE GAS

Another fine old converted music hall that's now an attractive venue for varied musical events. Jazz and salsa predominate.
✚ G6 ⊠ Muntaner 246 ☎ 93 486 44 22 Ⓜ Diagonal

THE QUIET MAN

One of the city's best Irish pubs has live Celtic music Thursday to Saturday.
✚ G9 ⊠ Marqués de Berbera 11 ☎ 93 412 12 19 ◻ Liceu

ZELESTE

House music alternates with big-name rock acts at this popular venue. Weekend club nights.
✚ K8 ⊠ Almogavers 122 ☎ 93 486 44 22 Ⓜ Marina

TRADITIONAL ENTERTAINMENT

DANCE VENUES

CENTRE ARTESÌ TRADICIONÀRIUS
Founded in 1993 for the study of traditional Catalan music, dance and instruments, this comfortable, intimate theatre presents frequent performances.
✚ H5 ✉ Travessera de Sant Antoni 6–8 ☎ 93 218 44 85 🚇 Fontana

L'ESPAI
On the edge of village-like Gràcia, the Space (full name: L'Espai de Dansa i Música de la Generalitat de Catalunya) is the regional government-subsidised venue for performances of traditional and modern dance.
✚ G5 ✉ Travessera de Gràcia 63 ☎ 93 201 29 06 🚇 Diagonal

EL PATIO ANDALUZ
Not native to Catalonia, flamenco was brought here by immigrants from southern Spain after the Civil War. It has now put down roots, so you can enjoy great performances at a number of places, of which this is one.
✚ G6 ✉ Aribau 242 ☎ 93 209 33 78 🚌 58, 64

SALA BECKETT
This small, subterranean Gràcia theatre serves as a performance space for many of the better dance companies
✚ J5 ✉ Alegre de Dalt 55 bis ☎ 93 284 53 12 🚇 Joanic

LOS TARANTOS
Here you will find some of the best flamenco acts in Catalonia. Conveniently located in Plaça Reial. You can dine while watching.
✚ G9 ✉ Plaça Reial 17 ☎ 93 318 59 66 🚇 Liceu

TABLAO DE CARMEN
This full-blooded flamenco show in touristy Poble Espanyol is none the worse for the setting – locals come here too. You can dine while watching the show, which is staged twice nightly.
✚ E8 ✉ Poble Espanyol ☎ 93 325 68 95 🚇 Espanya 🚌 13, 61

DANCE HALL

LA PALOMA
Robustly old-fashioned dance hall from the turn of the 20th century, with music to suit its wonderful mix of patrons from grandparents to grunge lovers.
✚ G8 ✉ Tigre 27 ☎ 93 301 68 97 🚇 Universitat

BULLRING

PLAÇA DE TOROS MONUMENTAL
Though it does have some following among native Catalans, bullfighting in Barcelona attracts mostly foreign tourists and visiting Spaniards. One of the city's big bull rings has now shut down; this one stages the corrida on spring and summer Sundays. It also has a museum, open during the bullfighting season (Apr–Sep).
✚ K7 ✉ Gran Via de les Corts Catalanes 749 ☎ 93 245 58 04 🚇 Monumental

Old-fashioned fun
El Molino, the most famous of Barcelona's music halls, may have closed down, but old-time cabaret and drag acts can still to be found at a few spots. The Bodega Bohèmia (Lancaster 2) is the haunt of cabaret artistes who refuse to retire, while the ageing drag queens of El Cangrejo (The Crab), at Corsega 36, have become an imperishable city institution.

LUXURY HOTELS

Prices

Expect to pay the following prices per night for a double room, but it's always worth asking when you make your reservation whether any special deals are available.

Budget	up to 15,000ptas
Mid-range	up to 25,000ptas
Luxury	over 25,000ptas

Booking accomodation

Barcelona is a great magnet for business visitors, and booking early is a must if you are to have much choice in where to stay. The Olympic building boom boosted the number of luxury hotels but also swept away some of the more modest accommodation. The concentration of hotels around the Rambla and within easy walking distance of Plaça de Catalunya makes this area of the city an obvious choice for first-time visitors.

ARTS BARCELONA
Up-to-the-minute luxury in two 44-storey towers – Spain's tallest buildings – overlooking the Port Olímpic. Opulent interiors and incomparable views.
✚ J9 ✉ Marina 19–21 ☎ 93 221 10 00 🚇 Ciutadella/Vila Olímpica

AVENIDA PALACE
Stands out for its central location and modern comforts despite what some might consider overly ornate decor.
✚ H7 ✉ Gran Via de les Corts Catalanes 605 ☎ 93 301 96 00 🚇 Passeig de Gràcia

CLARIS
This late 19th-century town house has become a hotel of the greatest refinement, with facilities ranging from several restaurants, fitness centre, Japanese garden, a rooftop terrace with pool, and a museum displaying priceless Egyptian antiquities.
✚ H7 ✉ Pau Claris 150 ☎ 93 487 62 62 🚇 Passeig de Gràcia

COLÓN
An enviable location opposite the cathedral makes the Colón a favourite. Specify a room up front, with a view of the cathedral, although the bells are very noisy.
✚ H8 ✉ Avinguda del Catedral 7 ☎ 93 301 14 04 🚇 Jaume I

CONDES DE BARCELONA
Within a handbag's throw of the prestigious boutiques and shops on the Passeig de Gràcia, this superb building has nearly 200 ultra-comfortable rooms furnished in *modernista* style.
✚ H7 ✉ Passeig de Gràcia 73–75 ☎ 93 488 22 00 🚇 Passeig de Gràcia, Diagonal

GRAN HOTEL CATALONIA
Discreet decor and a central position make the Catalonia an excellent choice at the lower end of this price category.
✚ G6 ✉ Balmes 142 ☎ 93 415 90 90 🚇 Provença

GRAN HOTEL HAVANA
An exceptional example of *modernista* architecture in the Eixample, the 145-room Havana is bold but tastefully decorated.
✚ H7 ✉ Gran Via de les Corts Catalanes ☎ 93 412 11 15 🚇 Passeig de Gràcia, Urquinaona

MERIDIEN BARCELONA
The superbly equipped Meridien profits from its proximity to the Liceu. Opera stars and business travellers alike enjoy its comforts and its superb position on the Rambla.
✚ G8 ✉ Rambla 111 ☎ 93 318 62 00 🚇 Liceu, Catalunya

RIVOLI RAMBLAS
This 87-room hotel dating from the 1930s has beautiful art-deco style and a terrace with a panorama over the Old City.
✚ G8 ✉ Rambla 128 ☎ 93 302 66 43 🚇 Catalunya

MID-RANGE HOTELS

ATLANTIS
Cleverly shoehorned into a narrow building barely more than one room thick, the Atlantis offers good value, more than adequate comfort, and an excellent location, though the back rooms overlook neighbouring skylights.
✚ G8 ✉ Pelai 20 ☎ 93 318 90 12 Ⓜ Catalunya

CITADINES BARCELONA RAMBLAS
In addition to modern hotel rooms, this establishment has studio and larger apartments available at budgetwise rates for longer periods. A rooftop terrace gives superb views over the city.
✚ G8 ✉ Rambla 122 ☎ 93 270 11 11 Ⓜ Catalunya

CONTINENTAL
On the upper floors of a building over-looking the top end of the Rambla, this comfortable hotel once harboured George Orwell and his wife in the days of the Civil War.
✚ H8 ✉ La Rambla 138 ☎ 93 301 25 70 Ⓜ Catalunya

DUQUES DE BERGARA
A prestigious edifice in *modernista* style in a fine location just off Plaça de Catalunya, offering great convenience and comfort.
✚ G8 ✉ Bergara 11 ☎ 93 301 51 51 Ⓜ Catalunya

GAUDÍ
No idle use of the great architect's name, this modern hotel has an enviable location directly opposite the Palau Güell, one of his masterworks.
✚ G9 ✉ Nou de la Rambla 12 ☎ 93 317 90 32 Ⓜ Liceu

GRANVIA
This medium-sized hotel is unmodernised but palatial and plush.
✚ H/ ✉ Gran Via de les Corts Catalanes 642 ☎ 93 318 19 00 Ⓜ Passeig de Gràcia

NOUVEL
A chance to stay in some comfort at very reasonable rates in one of the charming narrow streets of the Barri Gòtic.
✚ H8 ✉ Santa Anna 20 ☎ 93 301 82 74 Ⓜ Catalunya

ORIENTE
At the somewhat seedy lower end of the Rambla, the mid-19th-century Oriente has long since ceased to be *the* place to stay in Barcelona, but its ornate public spaces and only slightly less alluring bedrooms continue to attract customers who like lodgings with some character. Previous guests include Hans Christian Andersen and Errol Flynn.
✚ G9 ✉ La Rambla 45 ☎ 93 302 25 58 Ⓜ Liceu, Drassanes

REDING
Excellent and modern accommodation in a side street close to Plaça de Catalunya.
✚ G8 ✉ Gravina 5–7 ☎ 93 412 10 97 Ⓜ Universitat

SUIZO
Comfortable rooms make the moderately sized and welcoming Suizo a good choice in the Barri Gòtic.
✚ H9 ✉ Plaça de l'Àngel 12 ☎ 93 310 61 08 Ⓜ Jaume I

Sleepless city
Beware of noise. Barcelona is not a quiet city, and many of its citizens never seem to go to bed. A room on the Rambla may have a wonderful view, but without super-efficient double-glazing, undisturbed slumber cannot be guaranteed. Accommodation overlooking an unglamorous neighbouring skylight may be less picturesque but could prove a wiser choice.

BUDGET ACCOMMODATION

Camping

Several campsites are within striking distance of Barcelona. The nearest is close to the airport at El Prat de Llobregat ✉ Cala Gogó, Carretera de La Platja ☎ 93 379 46 00 🖶 65, from Plaça d'Espanya.

ESPAÑA

The glory days of the España may be over, but the interiors of this turn-of-the-20th-century *modernista* edifice just off the Rambla – decorated by some of the finest artists of the time – stand out still.

➕ G9 ✉ Sant Pau 9 ☎ 93 318 17 58 🚇 Liceu

GÒTICO

A well-established and comfortable choice in the centre of the Barri Gòtic. Upper end of the range.

➕ H9 ✉ Jaume I 14 ☎ 93 315 22 11 🚇 Jaume I

HOSTAL OLIVA

Barcelona's swankiest street is not so exclusive that it is impossible to stay on it without paying a fortune. Here are bargain rooms, some with just a washbasin, in a 16-room *hostal* on the top floor of an Eixample apartment block.

➕ H7 ✉ Passeig de Gràcia 32 ☎ 93 488 01 62 🚇 Passeig de Gràcia

INTERNACIONAL

The front rooms of this mid-sized hotel have a bird's-eye view of the Rambla with its brightly-coloured paving pattern by Joan Miró. Noise from the youth tour groups that favour the place may rival that from the busy street outside.

➕ G9 ✉ Rambla 78–80 ☎ 93 302 25 66 🚇 Liceu

MESON DE CASTILLA

If you're tired of Catalan *Modernisme*, check out this convincing re-creation of Castilian style in a side-street close to Plaça de Catalunya.

➕ G8 ✉ Valldoncella 5 ☎ 93 318 21 82 🚇 Universitat, Catalunya

PASEO DE GRÀCIA

A corner site at the upper end of the city's most prestigious avenue and fine views from the upper rooms make this simple hotel an excellent budget choice.

➕ H6 ✉ Passeig de Gràcia 102 ☎ 93 215 58 24

PELAYO

These idiosyncratic upper-floor lodgings, located through an entrance hall shared with other establishments, feel more like someone's slightly chaotic home. But the place is perfectly adequate, and it's convenient to Plaça de Catalunya.

➕ G8 ✉ Pelai 9 ☎ 93 302 37 27 🚇 Catalunya, Universitat

REY DON JAIME I

This small, welcoming hotel has an excellent location in the Barri Gòtic as well as rooms with private bath at very reasonable prices.

➕ H9 ✉ Jaume I 11 ☎ 93 310 62 08 🚇 Jaume I

ROMA REIAL

A simple place overlooking the elegant Plaça Reial.

➕ G9 ✉ Plaça Reial 11 ☎ 93 302 03 36 🚇 Licéu

TAMASHIRO

Basic but adequate accommodation in a street that runs off the Rambla into the Raval.

➕ G8 ✉ Hospital 93 ☎ 93 329 54 87 🚇 Liceu

BARCELONA
travel facts

Arriving & Departing   *88–89*

Essential Facts   *89–90*

Public Transport   *90–91*

Media & Communications   *91–92*

Emergencies   *92–93*

Language   *93*

Arriving & Departing

Before you go

- Anyone entering Spain must have a valid passport (or official identity card for EU nationals).
- Nationals of Australia and South Africa require a valid passport plus visa.
- Take form E111 from the Post Office before going to cover emergency medical treatment.
- Take out full health and travel insurance before travelling.

When to go

- Barcelona has no off-season – there is always something to see and do. But late spring (May and early June) and early autumn (late September and early October) are ideal visiting times.

Climate

- Hot and humid high summer. Mild winter.
- Annual average temperature 15.8° C (January 10°, August 25°).
- Occasional heavy rain, any season.

Arriving by air

- Barcelona's modernised airport is at El Prat de Llobregat, 12km from the city. Terminal A serves non-Spanish airlines, Terminal B serves Iberia international flights ☎ 93 298 38 38
- Barcelona is served by 32 international airlines and has direct flights to more than 80 international destinations.
- Trains link the airport with Sants, Plaça de Catalunya, Arc de Triomf and Clot-Aragó stations. They run every 30 minutes and the journey time to Plaça de Catalunya is 25 minutes.
- The convenient Aerobus service links both terminals with Plaça de Catalunya via Plaça d'Espanya

and Gran Via de les Corts (and Sants station for travel to the airport). The service operates every 20 minutes in both directions, from early morning until at least 10PM. The journey time is about 30 minutes.

Arriving by train

- Barcelona is connected by direct train with major cities in Spain and with a number of destinations in other European countries.
- The Estació de França near Barceloneta has trains to Paris, Geneva, Zürich and Milan as well as local trains.
- Sants station in the west of the city centre has direct trains to Montpellier in France with TGV connections to Paris as well as local trains and a direct connection to the metro.
- Many main-line trains run beneath the city centre stopping at the underground stations at Passeig de Gràcia and Plaça de Catalunya.
- Rail information: National ☎ 93 490 02 02; International ☎ 93 490 11 22

Arriving by bus

- Direct coach services operate from several European countries including Britain.
- Main bus station: Estació d'Autobusos Barcelona Nord ☎ 93 265 65 08

Arriving by car

- Barcelona is connected by the A7 toll *autopista* to the French frontier and motorway network at La Jonquera (150km north-east).
- Toulouse is 388km north via N152, the French frontier at Puigcerdà and RN20.
- Motorway access to the rest of Spain is via *autopistas* A2 and A7.
- Car ferry services from Britain to Spain are operated by Brittany

Ferries (Plymouth–Santander) and by P&O European Ferries (Portsmouth–Bilbao).

Arriving by sea

- Ferry services operate to the Balearic Islands from the Port of Barcelona ☎ 93 443 13 00. One of the largest ferry operators is Trasmediterranea ☎ 93 295 91 00

Customs regulations

- There is no limit on the importation of tax-paid goods purchased by EU nationals within the European Union if they are for personal use.
- The limits for non-EU visitors are 200 cigarettes or 100 small cigars or 250g of tobacco; 1 litre of alcohol (over 22 percent alcohol) or 2 litre of fortified wine; 50g of perfume.
- Residents of non-EU countries may be able to claim back the Value Added Tax on purchases made in Spain.

Airport tax

- The cost of your air ticket normally includes airport tax.

ESSENTIAL FACTS

Electricity

- 220/225 volts AC with standard European two-pin plug. (In some places 110/125 volts AC.)

Etiquette

- It's normal to wish people *bon dia* (good day), and hands are shaken frequently.
- Expect to find unabashed smokers in public places.
- Do not wear shorts, short skirts, or skimpy tops in churches.

Lone and women travellers

- Barcelona is a reasonably female-friendly city, certainly compared with southern Spain. Women are unlikely to be hassled.
- Among a number of feminist organisations is Ca La Dona ✉ Carrer Casp 38 ☎ 93 412 71 61

Money matters

- The unit of currency is the Spanish peseta (pta, ptas) which comes in the form of coins (1, 5, 10, 25, 50, 100, 200 and 500) and notes (1000, 2000, 5000, and 10,000).
- The euro became the official currency of Spain on 1 January 1999 and the peseta became a denomination of the euro. Peseta notes and coins continue to be legal tender until euro banknotes and coins are introduced on 1 January 2002.
- Foreign currency and travellers' cheques can be changed at banks and bureau de change. Rates vary and should be compared. It may be best to use cash machines
- Major credit cards are in wide use.

National holidays

- 1 January; 6 January (Three Kings); Good Friday; Easter Monday; 1 May; Whit Monday; 24 June (St John); 15 August (Assumption); 11 September (Catalan National Day); 24 September (Our Lady of Mercy); 12 October (Discovery of America); 1 November (All Saints); 6 December (Constitution Day); 8 December (Immaculate Conception); 25 and 26 December.

Opening hours

- Bank hours: Mon–Fri 8:30–2 and, except in summer, Sat too, though there are many local variations.
- Shops: Mon–Sat 9 or 10–1:30, 4:30–7:30 (hours are variable). Larger shops and department stores may open all day. Some Sunday opening.

89

- Restaurants: lunch 2–4, dinner 9–midnight (hours vary, and restaurants in tourist areas often open earlier for lunch and dinner).
- Museums shut for the lunch-time siesta and close early on Sunday.

Places of worship
- Anglican: St George's Church ✉ Horaci 38 ☎ 93 417 88 67 ⏰ Service Sun 11AM
- Mass in English: Parròquia Maria Reina ✉ Carretera d'Esplugues 103 ☎ 93 203 41 15 ⏰ Mass Sun 10AM

Student travellers
- Barcelona is youth-friendly, with a large student population and numerous hostels and youth hotels.
- Reduced admission to many museums with student card.
- Information on youth activities available from: Àrea de Asuntos Sociales y Juventud ✉ Carrer Ferran 32 ☎ 93 402 78 00
- Viva Youth and Student Travel: ✉ Carrer Rocafort 116–122 ☎ 93 483 83 81

Time differences
- Spain is two hours ahead of Greenwich Mean Time in summer, and one hour ahead in winter.

Toilets
- Public toilets are comparatively rare, though there are a number of French-style street cubicles. However, *servicios* can usually be found in large department stores or museums. Otherwise, try to synchronise your needs with breaks in cafés and restaurants.

Tourist offices
- Centre d'Informació, Plaça de Catalunya. Main centre of the city's tourist board. Large underground premises with hotel booking, bureau de change and souvenir and bookshop ⏰ daily 9–9
- Other information centres at Sants railway station, Congress Palace, and (summer only) booths on the Rambla (harbour end), Passeig de Gràcia (corner with Carrer Aragó) and at Sagrada Familia.
- Uniformed tourist officials known as 'Red Jackets' patrol popular tourist areas in summer.
- Officines d'Informació Turística. Catalan Government tourist offices, at airport terminals A and B. Emphasis on regional information.
- Information on cultural events: Centre d'Informació de la Virreina. ✉ Palau de la Virreina, Rambla 99

Visitors with disabilities
- Provision for people with disabilities is reasonable and slowly improving.
- Most newer buildings and some bus routes have excellent facilities. Older establishments are likely to present problems.
- Institut Municipal de Disminüits ✉ Carrer Comte d'Urgell 240 ☎ 93 407 13 47 (city organisation responsible for promoting the interests of the disabled).

PUBLIC TRANSPORT

Although Barcelona is a walker's city *par excellence*, at some point you will need to use the first-rate system of integrated public transport, based on bus and metro and supplemented by a number of oddities like funiculars and the last remaining tram line, the Tramvia Blau. One underground line of the regional railway (FGC) is in effect part of the metro network, but whereas a single metro ticket enables you to travel anywhere on the system, you must use an additional ticket for the FGC.

Pick up a map of the network from a tourist information centre or one of the TMB (Metropolitan Transport Corporation) offices; these are in the metro stations at Plaça de la Universitat, Barcelona-Sants and Sagrada Familia.

- Public transport information line: ☎ 010

Types of ticket

Single tickets are available, but it makes sense to pay for multiple journeys by one of several types of *targeta* (travelcard):

- *Targeta* 1 valid for 10 trips by metro (and FGC) or bus.
- *Targeta* 50/30 valid for 50 trips by metro (and FGC).
- You must cancel one unit of a *targeta* per journey undertaken by inserting it into the automatic machine at the entry to a station or aboard a bus. The *targeta* can be shared by a group of people.
- Passes for unlimited bus and metro use are available for 1 day, 3 days and 5 days.

Metro

- There are five lines, identified by number and colour.
- Direction is indicated by the name of the station at the end of the line.
- The network covers most (but not all) parts of the city and is still being extended.
- The metro runs Mon–Thu 5AM–11PM, Fri, Sat and the evening before public holidays 5AM–1AM, and Sun 6AM–midnight.

Buses

- Bus is the the most convenient way of reaching some important parts of the city.
- The free *Guía d'Autobusos Urbans de Barcelona* details routes.
- More information (including

frequency of service) is given on the panels at bus stops.

- Buses mostly run 6:30AM–10PM.
- There is a special (more expensive) night service, the Nitbus, with routes centred on Plaça de Catalunya.
- Useful tourist routes include numbers 22 (Plaça de Catalunya-Gràcia-Tramvia Blau-Pedralbes Monastery) and 24 (Plaça de Catalunya-Gràcia-Parc Güell).
- The Bus Turístic operates two routes, north and south, giving the best view of the city, including all the main sights.

Taxi

- Barcelona's fleet of taxis numbers 11,000. Their black and yellow livery makes them a familiar sight in the street scene.
- They can be hailed when displaying a green light and the sign *Lliure/Libre* (free), or can be picked up at a number of taxi ranks.
- Fares are not unduly expensive.
- There are several phone cab firms ☎ 93 358 11 11/ 93 392 22 22/ 93 490 22 22/ 93 433 10 20

MEDIA & COMMUNICATIONS

Telephones

- New public phones accept coins, phonecards and credit cards.
- Older types only accept coins (minimum 20ptas).
- Phonecards (*credifone*) are available from tobacconists.
- Calls are cheaper after 10PM on weekdays, after 2PM Saturday and all day Sunday.
- National operator ☎ 1009
- International operator: Europe ☎ 1008; elsewhere ☎ 1005
- Directory enquiries ☎ 1003
- International directory enquiries ☎ 025

- Telephone numbers listed in this guide include the Barcelona area code (☎ 93). You must dial this code, even within Barcelona itself.
- To phone Spain from the UK dial 0034, followed by the number you want to reach, including the relevent city code. For example, to call the British consulate in Barcelona, dial 0034 93 419 90 44.
- Telegrams ☎ 93 322 24 96

Post offices

- Main post office (Correu Central) ✉ Plaça Antoni López ☎ 902 1971 97 🕔 Mon–Fri 8AM–10PM; Sat 9AM–8PM; Sun 9AM–1PM 🚇 Barceloneta. Address poste restante correspondence to Lista de Correos, 08070, Barcelona.
- Other central post offices are at Plaça Bonsuccès, Ronda Universitat 23, and Carrer València 231.
- Stamps are for sale at tobacconists.
- Postboxes are coloured Spanish blood and sand (yellow and red).

Newspapers

- Many international papers arrive on the day of publication and can be found in the kiosks on the Rambla and Passeig de Gràcia.
- Papers published in Barcelona include the top seller *La Vanguardia* (Spanish – conservative, with listings supplement), *Avui* (Catalan – nationalist) and *El País* (Spanish – leftish, with listings supplement).
- The English-language monthly *Barcelona Metropolitan*, launched 1996 (free), has some listings.
- The main listings periodical is the weekly *Guía del Ocio*.
- *Top Tips Barcelona* is a free periodical full of advertising.

Radio

- BBC World Service on 15070, 12095, 9410 and 6195 Short Wave.

Television

- Local television includes TVE 1 (Spanish) and TVE 2 (Spanish and Catalan), both national channels, and TV3 (Catalan).
- The more expensive hotels have satellite TV with a mixture of international channels.

EMERGENCIES

Emergency phone numbers

- Guardia Urbana (City police) ☎ 092
- Policía Nacional (National police) ☎ 091
- Ambulance ☎ 061
- Fire ☎ 080
- Turisme-Atenció (tourist assistance) ☎ 93 301 90 60

Consulates

- Australia ✉ Gran Via Carles III 98 ☎ 93 330 94 96
- Canada ✉ Travessera de les Corts, 265 ☎ 93 215 07 04
- Ireland ✉ Gran Via Carles III 94 ☎ 93 491 50 21
- New Zealand ✉ Travessera de Gràcia 64 ☎ 93 209 03 99
- United Kingdom ✉ Diagonal 477 ☎ 93 419 90 44
- United States ✉ Passeig Reina Elisenda 23 ☎ 93 280 22 27

Lost property

- Servei de Troballes ✉ Ajuntament, Carrer Ciutat 9 ☎ 93 402 31 61

Medical treatment

- EU citizens are entitled to free medical treatment if in possession of Form E111, available from home post offices prior to travel.
- Public hospitals will provide free treatment in the case of a genuine emergency.
- City centre casualty department (*urgències*): ✉ Centre d'Urgències Perecamps, Avinguda de les Drassanes 13–15 ☎ 93 441 06 00 🚇 Drassanes

- Check with your consulate to find private foreign-language doctors and medical treatment.
- Pharmacies (*Farmàcies*) offer a wider range of treatments and medicines than in many countries.
- Pharmacy opening hours Mon–Sat 9–1:30, 4:30–8. Rota operated at other times.

Sensible precautions

- Any place frequented by tourists may attract pickpockets. The lower end of the Rambla and the Raval area have a reputation for this type of activity, but it can happen anywhere.
- Carry valuables in a money-belt or pouch, not in a pocket.
- Wear bags across the front of your body, not over the shoulder. Keep wearing bags and cameras when seated and keep an eye on belongings in cafés and bars.
- Beware teams of operators: one may engage you in conversation while another removes your valuables to pass them on to yet another colleague.

LANGUAGE

- Suppressed until after the death of Franco in 1975, Catalan now enjoys equal status to Spanish in Barcelona and Catalonia and must *not* be thought of as a dialect. It is also the language of the Valencia region, the Balearic Islands, and the Rousillon area of France.
- Street signs and official communications are now mostly in Catalan, but virtually everyone understands Spanish, which is also the language of tourism.
- Most people in the tourist industry speak some English and French.
- Any effort to speak Spanish or (especially) Catalan will be welcomed, though do not be too disappointed if your attempt at Catalan is thought to be mispronounced Spanish!

English	*Spanish/Catalan*
good morning	buenos días/ bon dia
good evening	buenas tardes/ bona tarda
good night	buenas noches/ bona nit
hello	hola/hola
goodbye	adiós/adéu
thank you	gracias/gràcies
you're welcome	de nada/de res
please	por favor/si us pla
yes, no	si, no/sí, no
open	abierto/obert
closed	cerrado/tancat
church	iglesia/església
museum	museo/museu
palace	palacio/palau
street	calle/carrer
toilet	aseos, servicios/ lavabo
Monday	lunes/dilluns
Tuesday	martes/dimarts
Wednesday	miércoles/ dimecres
Thursday	jueves/dijous
Friday	viernes/ divendres
Saturday	sábado/dissabte
Sunday	domingo/ diumenge
1, 2	un (uno/una), dos/un (una), dos
3, 4	tres, cuatro/tres, quatre
5, 6	cinco, seis/cinc, sis
7, 8	siete, ocho/set, vuit
9, 10	nueve, diez/nou, deu

INDEX

A

accommodation 84-6
airport 88
airport tax 89
Ajuntament 41
anarchy 12, 37
antiques shops 77
Aquarium 44
Arc de Triomf 17, 46
Arsenal 47
arts, crafts and design
    shops 71

B

banks 89
Barceloneta 15, 18, 48
Barri Gòtic 7, 15, 18, 60, 71
bars 68-69, 78-9
beach 9, 48, 60
Betlem 57
boat trips 19
bookshops 75
Boqueria market 14, 76
bullrings 83
Bus Turístic 19, 91
buses 91
buses, long-distance 88

C

Caballé, Montserrat 8
Cadafalch, Puig i 7, 33
cafés 68-69
camping 86
Carrer dels Escudellers 18
Carrer de Montcada 17
Casa Amatller 33
Casa Batlló 33
Casa Comalat 52
Casa Fuster 15, 26, 52
Casa Lleó-Morera 33
Casa Macaya 52
Casa Milà 14, 32
Casa Museu Gaudí 27
Casa Terrades 52
Casa Vicens 26, 52
Casals, Pau 80
Catalonia 6, 7, 9, 12
Catedral 15, 39
Centre de Cultura
    Contemporània 34
Ceramics Museum 24, 60
Cerdà, Ildefons 12, 33
Chapel of St Agatha 40
children's attractions 59
churches 57
Cimenteri del Sud-est 28
cinemas 80
Citadel 16-17, 46

City History Museum 40, 60
Civil War 12, 42, 56, 57
climate 88
clubs 78-9
Columbus Column 35, 44
communications 91-2
consulates 92
Contemporary Art,
    Museum of 34
Costa Brava 58
Costa Daurada 58
credit cards 89
crime 93
currency 89
customs regulations 89

D

dance venues 83
disabilities, visitors with 90
discos 78-9
Drassanes 14, 36
drinking water 69
driving to Barcelona 88-9

E

eating out 62-9
Eixample 6, 12, 14, 16, 72
electricity 89
emergencies 92-3
emergency phone numbers
    92
entertainment 78-83
Espai Gaudí 32
Estadi Olímpic 58
etiquette 89
evening strolls 18
excursions 20-1
Expo 1929 28, 53

F

fashion shops 72–3
ferry services 89
festivals and events 22, 26
film 80
flamenco 83
Franco, General 11, 24
Frederic Marès Museum
    51, 60
free attractions 60
Fundació Antoni Tàpies
    14, 50
Fundació Joan Miró 15, 31
funiculars 59

G

Galera Real 36
Galeria Olímpica 58

galleries and museums 50-1
Gaudí, Antoni 6, 12, 24, 26,
    27, 32, 33, 37, 46, 52, 56
geography 9
gifts and souvenirs 74, 77
Girona 21
golondrines 19, 59
Gothic Quarter see Barri
    Gòtic
Gràcia 6, 15, 26
guided tours 19

H

history 10-12
Hospital de la Santa Creu i
    Sant Pau 15, 52-3
hotels 84-6

I

Ictíneo 50
IMAX 44
insurance 88
itineraries 14-15

J

jazz venues 82

L

language 6, 93
Llorens, Martí 8
lone travellers 89
lost property 92

M

malls and department
    stores 70
Manzana de la Discòrdia
    14, 33
Maragall, Pasqual 8
Maremagnum 19, 44
markets 35, 76, 77
media 92
medical treatment 92-3
de la Mercé 57
metro 91
Mies van der Rohe germany
    Pavilion 28, 53
Miró, Joan 31, 35, 55
modern architecture 52-3
Modern Art, Museum of 47
Modernisme 6, 7, 24, 33,
    47, 52, 53
money 89
Montaner, Domènech i 7,
    26, 33, 38
Montjuïc 15, 28
Montserrat 20
Monument a Colom 44

Muntanya Màgica 59
Museu d'Art
    Contemporani 34
Museu d'Art Modern 47
Museu de les Arts
    Decoratives 24
Museu Capitular 39
Museu de Cera 14, 59
Museu de Ceràmica 24, 60
Museu de la Ciencia i de la
    Tècnica 51
Museu d'Història de la
    Ciutat 40, 60
Museu d'Història de
    Catalunya 15, 45
Museu Marítim 36
Museu Monestir de
    Pedralbes 14, 25, 60
Museu Nacional d'Art de
    Catalunya 15, 30
Museu del Perfum 16, 51
Museu Picasso 42, 60
Museu Romàntic 21
Museu Tèxtil i
    d'Indumentària 51, 60
Museu de Vi 21
museum opening hours 89
music 38, 75, 80, 82
music hall 83

N
national holidays 89
newspapers 22, 92
nightlife 78-9
Nou Camp 58

O
Olympic Games 7, 28, 48
opening hours 89

P
Palau de la Generalitat 41
Palau de la Música
    Catalana 17, 38
Palau de Mar 17, 45
Palau Güell 14, 53
Palau Nacional 28, 30
Palau de Pedralbes 24
Palau de Sant Jordi 28
Parc d'Atraccions de
    Montjuïc 58
Parc d'Atraccions de
    Tibidabo 59
Parc de la Ciutadella 17,
    46, 59
Parc del Clot 54
Parc de la Creueta del Coll
    54

Parc de l'Espanya
    Industrial 54
Parc del Fossar de la
    Pedrera 54
Parc Güell 15, 26, 27, 60
Parc Joan Miró 55
Parc del Laberint d'Horta
    54-5
parks and gardens 54-5, 60
passports 88
Pedralbes Monastery 25, 60
pharmacies 93
Picasso Museum 42, 60
Picasso, Pablo 12, 42
picnic food 76
Plaça de Catalunya 7, 16, 56
Plaça Diamant 26
Plaça dels Països Catalans 55
Plaça Ramon Berenguer el
    Gran 40
Plaça del Rei 40
Plaça Reial 18, 56
Plaça Rius i Taulet 26, 56
Plaça Sant Jaume 14, 40, 41
Plaça Sant Pere 17
Plaça del Sol 26, 56
Plaça Virreina 26
plaças 56
places of worship 90
Poble Espanyol 29, 60, 77
police 92
population 9
Port Olímpic 48
Port Vell 44
post offices 92
public transport 9, 90-1
Pujol, Jordi 8
Pyrenees 58

R
radio and television 92
Rambla 6, 14, 18, 35, 60
Rambla de Mar 44
restaurants 62-9
Ribera 43

S
safety 93
Sagrada Familia 15, 37
Sanchez-Vicario, Arantxa 8
Sant Miquel del Port 57
Sant Pau del Camp 57
Sant Sadurní d'Anoia 21
Santa Maria del Mar 15, 17,
    43
Santa Maria del Pi 18, 57
sardana 39, 41, 60
Science and Technology,

    Museum of 51
sculpture 60
seafood 63, 67
Sentimental Museum 51
Sert, Josep-Luis 31
shoes and accessories 74
shopping 70-7, 89
Sierra de Collserola 7
sightseeing, organised 19
Sitges 20-1
smoking etiquette 89
Spanish Village 29, 60, 77
sports and amusements 58
statistics 9
street performers 60
student travellers 90

T
tapas bars 68-9
Tàpies, Antoni 8, 50
taxes 66
taxis 91
telephones 91-2
Textiles and Fashion,
    Museum of 51, 60
theatre 26, 80, 81
Thyssen-Bornemisza
    collection 14, 25
time differences 90
tipping 66
toilets 90
tourist offices 90
traditional entertainment 83
train services 88
Tramvia Blau 59
travellers' cheques 89
travelling to Barcelona 88-9
trees in the city 55

U
useful words and phrases 93

V
Velodrom de Horta 58
Vilafranca del Penedés 21
visas 88

W
walks 16-18
waterfront 14, 17, 44, 48
Wax Museum 59
Wine Museum 21
women travellers 89

Z
Zoo 46, 59
Zoological Museum 17, 46,
    53

CityPack
Barcelona

Written by   Michael Ivory
Edited, designed and produced by
 [AA] Publishing
Maps   © The Automobile Association 1997, 2000
Fold-out map © RV Reise- und Verkehrsverlag Munich · Stuttgart
 © Cartography: GeoData

Distributed in the United Kingdom by AA Publishing, Norfolk House, Priestley Road, Basingstoke, Hampshire, RG24 9NY.

The contents of this publication are believed correct at the time of printing. Nevertheless, the publishers cannot be held responsible for any errors or omissions or for changes in the details given in this guide or for the consequences of any reliance on the information provided by the same. Assessments of attractions, hotels, restaurants and so forth are based upon the author's own personal experience and, therefore, descriptions given in this guide necessarily contain an element of subjective opinion which may not reflect the publishers' opinion or dictate a reader's own experiences on another occasion.
We have tried to ensure accuracy in this guide, but things do change and we would be grateful if readers would advise us of any inaccuracies they may encounter.

Acknowledgements

The author would like to thank Mana-Luisa Albacar of Turisme de Barcelona for her help and kindness in the preparation of this book, Richard Schweid of Barcelona Metro, and Ingham's Travel of London for help in speeding him to his destination.
The Automobile Association would like to thank the following photographers, libraries and museums for their assistance in the preparation of this book:
Museu National d'Art Catalunya 30,30b; Museu d'Art Contemporani 34; Museu Picasso 12,42; Museu d'Art Modern 47; Rex Features 8; Spectrum Colour Library 38a; World Pictures cover (dancers). The remaining pictures are held in the association's own photo library (AA PHOTO LIBRARY) and were taken by Steve Day with the exception of the following pages which were taken by Philip Enticnap 18,19, 21 and Peter Wilson 1, 9, 20, 29b, 31b, 33, 36a, 36b, 37b, 38b, 39, 41b, 43a, 43b, 45b, 46b, 49b, 51b.

AUTHOR *Michael Ivory*
SECOND EDITION UPDATED BY *Kevin Fylan*
INDEXER *Marie Lorimer*

Titles in the CityPack series
● Amsterdam ● Atlanta ● Bangkok ● Beijing ● Berlin ● Boston ● Brussels & Bruges ●
● Chicago ● Dublin ● Florence ● Hong Kong ● Istanbul ● Lisbon ● London ●
● Los Angeles ● Madrid ● Miami ● Montréal ● Moscow ● Munich ● New York ●
● Paris ● Prague ● Rome ● San Francisco ● Seattle ● Singapore ● Shanghai ●
● Sydney ● Tokyo ● Toronto ● Venice ● Vienna ● Washington ●